TAKE FIVE

ON-THE-JOB MEDITATIONS WITH ST. IGNATIUS

TAKE FIVE

ON-THE-JOB MEDITATIONS WITH ST. IGNATIUS

MIKE AQUILINA & FR. KRIS D. STUBNA

Our Sunday Visitor Publishing Division
Our Sunday Visitor, Inc.
Huntington, Indiana 46750

Nihil Obstat:
Rev. Michael Heintz
Censor Librorum

Imprimatur:
✠ John M. D'Arcy
Bishop of Fort Wayne-South Bend
December 27, 2007

The *Nihil Obstat* and *Imprimatur* are declarations that a work is free from doctrinal or moral error. It is not implied that those who have granted the *Nihil Obstat* and *Imprimatur* agree with the contents, opinions, or statements expressed.

Contents

Foreword *by Father Raymond Gawronski, S.J.*   8
Introduction   10
    How to Use This Book   10
    The Life of Ignatius   12
    The Spirit of Ignatius   20
References   27

The Meditations

1. The World Needs You   29
2. Use the Gifts God Gave You   31
3. Prayer for Generosity   33
4. Higher Goals, Better Striving   35
5. Work: A Continuous Prayer   37
6. Keep the Goal in Mind   38
7. God Is Here   40
8. How to Win Friends and Influence People   42
9. Don't Procrastinate   44
10. Extra Effort   46
11. Modesty in All Things   48
12. Speak Moderately and Politely   50
13. The Benefit of the Doubt   52
14. Correcting Others   54
15. Instructions on Dealing With Others   56
16. Learn to Listen   58
17. On Flatterers and Friends   60
18. Work for Peace   62
19. Take Time for Self-Improvement   64

20. First Things First   66
21. Decision Making   68
22. On Time   70
23. Making Sacrifices for Others   72
24. Speaking of Co-workers   74
25. Office Gossip   75
26. Idle Talk   77
27. When Co-workers Are Downhearted   79
28. Be a Peacemaker   81
29. That All Might Be Saved   83
30. Good Deeds: You *Can* Take Them With You   85
31. Work With What You Have   87
32. People Before Paychecks   89
33. Setting the Standard   91
34. To Speak Up or Keep Silent?   94
35. Obeying the Teaching Church   96
36. Menial Work   98
37. Keep Busy and Out of Trouble   100
38. Asking for a Raise   102
39. Against Presumption   104
40. Nothing's Going Right!   106
41. How God Teaches   108
42. Courage!   110
43. Don't Overdo It   112
44. Sick Days   114
45. Take Care of Yourself   116
46. The Grass Seems Greener Over There   118
47. Self-Pity and Discouragement   120
48. Anxiety About Spiritual Things   122
49. When We Are Ashamed   124

50. Don't Blame Others 126
51. The Temptation of the Future 128
52. Encourage Your Critics 129
53. Friends 130
54. The Name of God 131
55. Make Time for Quiet 133
56. Never Alone 135
57. We Are Not Hermits 136
58. Seeing Clearly 138
59. Driving Out Vice 139
60. Back to the Basics 140
61. Praying the Lord's Prayer 142
62. Receive Jesus Often 144
63. Say "Thanks" 146
64. Fair Wages! 148
65. Cross Examination 150
66. Holy Indifference 153
67. The Things of This World 155
68. False Humility 157
69. Give as God Has Given 159
70. Prayer Goes to Work 161
71. The Circle of Service and Prayer 163
72. Contemplation in Action 165
73. Aim High 167
74. A.M.D.G. 169

Index 171
About the Authors 175

Foreword

St. Thomas Aquinas teaches that the contemplative life is to be preferred to the active, but that the mixed life is better than both, as the fruits of contemplation can serve our neighbor. This "mixed life" characterizes the vocation of St. Ignatius of Loyola, whose followers soon saw themselves as "contemplatives in action." Resisting the natural attraction of permanent withdrawal from the world, St. Ignatius insisted that God can be found in the midst of the world itself.

The key to "finding God in all things" for this tradition was not spending long periods of time in secluded prayer, but rather in mortification. That is to say, formation in the proper ascetical discipline can progressively free the disciple of Christ from inordinate attachments in order to be ever more conformed to the Master, able to let his life be molded by God into a likeness of Jesus. Aided by grace, the world itself becomes the "theater of God's glory," where, by spiritual sobriety, one watches for the action of God's grace and learns to cooperate with it.

Take Five is a very rich collection of gems from the very practical yet profound wisdom of St. Ignatius of Loyola, one of the greatest spiritual masters the world has known. The authors have mined the deep veins of St. Ignatius's many writings to present a most helpful and balanced overview of what it is to be an active apostle in the marketplace. It is a work that Jesuits have been doing for centuries: that is, helping people

8

in the world order their lives according to God's plan to live the mission that God shares with us in Jesus. Now, in our time, which has been rediscovering the mystical dimension of the spiritual life, *Take Five* offers a fine, solid, and much needed help toward laying the ascetical foundation that is the key to "finding God in all things."

FATHER RAYMOND GAWRONSKI, S.J.

Father Gawronski is a member of the Maryland Province, a professor and spiritual director at St. John Vianney Seminary in Denver, and the author of A Closer Walk with Christ *(Our Sunday Visitor).*

How to Use This Book

Most Christians spend a large part of their waking hours in activity related to their professional work. They put in long shifts — on the shop floor, in the classroom, in the office — and they pass even more time commuting to and from their labors. Thus, when they pass from this life, they will likely be judged to a great extent on what they did for a living.

Yet so many sermons and books on the spiritual life seem to pass over these everyday realities and focus instead on matters that are important — methods of meditation, volunteer work, almsgiving — but that hold a marginal place in the ordinary days of ordinary people.

In this book, we bring the rich teachings of St. Ignatius of Loyola (1491-1556) to bear on the everyday circumstances of working life. Ignatius worked prodigiously through his life, and he urged his friends and followers to do the same. Yet he was always able to see the supernatural dimension of his tasks, even when they were mundane, difficult, or demanding of his entire attention.

How was he able to stay focused? He found very practical ways to bring Christ into the workday, and he shared his methods with others. He wrote letters full of good advice about getting work done, and doing it with care, yet not wearying yourself; about getting along with co-workers; about dealing with office politics; and about the challenge of keeping your eye on the goal, which is not worldly success but godly glory. These spiritual counsels, along with occasional anecdotes from the biographies of Ignatius, make up the bulk of the book's meditations.

Even if our lives do not reproduce Ignatius's material success, we can still achieve the (more important) spiritual goals that God has set for our work. This is what God wants; and God is all-powerful; so He will give us all we need to succeed.

The best way to learn from Ignatius is to get to know him first as a person and a teacher. Please begin by reading the story of his life, provided below, which is followed by the brief sketch of his spirituality.

The meditations may be read in any sequence that suits you. They do follow a certain logic, moving from elementary to ultimate matters. But you may find it occasionally useful to jump around in search of the subject that occupies your mind.

Each meditation begins with an excerpt from Ignatius's writings. Historical or other background is provided when needed.

The meditation proceeds to a short section titled "**Think About It**." There are a few points listed for you to consider in your prayer. You may refer them to yourself in God's presence, or refer them to God for answers, or both. Take time with each point. Don't rush. Wait quietly and patiently for God's response in your soul. He will not fail you — though His response may not be immediately sensible to you. Sometimes many years go by before we can see how God worked in our soul in prayer at a given moment.

Next is a short section called "**Just Imagine**." A brief passage from Scripture is provided, usually from the

Gospels or the letters of the apostles. Ignatius teaches us to try to enter these biblical scenes as a participant or an onlooker so that we can personally experience the touch of Jesus, the teaching of Paul, and so on. Use your imagination!

Finally, on each page, you'll see a brief line or two with the heading "**Remember**." Copy this line onto a piece of paper and take it with you to work. Pull it out of your pocket occasionally and repeat it as a prayer. See if you can pray it from memory by the end of the day.

Try to build time into your schedule so that you can pray one meditation — or pray without these meditations — for at least twenty minutes each day, preferably in the morning. Our relationship with God, like any personal relationship, grows deeper through conversation: intimate, heart-to-heart conversation. Workaholics look upon conversation as a luxury, but they're wrong. It is as necessary as drawing breath. It makes us human. And when our conversation is prayer, it makes us divine.

You wouldn't leave home without the tools of your trade. Try not to leave home without your morning prayer.

The Life of Ignatius

In 1491, at the castle of Loyola, near the town of Azpeitia in the Basque region of Spain, a prominent noble family received a surprise from God. The surprise was the arrival of their eleventh child, a son whom they named Iñigo, but whom later generations would know as Ignatius. It was a custom at that time for noble families to dedicate their youngest child to the service of the Church, and the Lord and the Lady — Don Beltrán de Loyola and Doña Marina Saenz de Licona — had already done so with their tenth child, Pero.

Then along came Ignatius; and this great family of Loyola, who were great in their passions, gave him to the Church as well. Some of their kinsmen held prominent positions in the local Church, which, perhaps, the parents hoped would fall to their young sons some day.

Passion and ambition had marked the character of the Loyolas for many generations, and theirs were not always the higher sort of longings and strivings. Court ledgers show that the men and women in Ignatius's bloodline were given to acts of vengeance, and they could sustain feuds for long stretches of time. Some were convicted of robbery. Many were prone to dueling and gang warfare; and occasionally they were charged with murder. Ignatius's father was no exception, having sired two children out of wedlock in addition to his eleven with Doña Marina.

Ignatius's mother died when he was a very small boy, but he received continuing maternal care from his peasant wet nurse and from the wife of his oldest brother, Martin.

Because his parents had dedicated him to the Church, Ignatius would have undergone the ritual of the tonsure at some point in his childhood. Boys destined for the priesthood or religious life were, from then on, marked by the distinctive short haircut that left them shaven at the crown of the head.

At that time in Spain, clergy received all sorts of privileges, including immunity from civil prosecution. These honors extended also to youngsters dedicated for the priesthood. So, when the young Ignatius got into trouble, he at least once invoked his clerical state to save his delinquent hide.

However, he seems to have given otherwise little thought to his supposed vocation, or even to living a minimally Christian life. He never stopped believing in the Catholic faith; indeed, he was even then attached to certain devotions. But he was more attached to worldly things; and, as he grew to young manhood, these were most often the objects of his passions.

In his teen years, Ignatius received a prestigious appointment. His father arranged for him to serve as a page in the household of Juan Velázquez de Cuéllar, a man very influential in the court of the king and queen of Spain. As a page, Ignatius would be trained in the ways of knighthood. Those who persevered in such training often went on to serve the throne in positions of power, either in the military or in government.

At some point, it seems, Ignatius had abandoned his dedication to the priesthood. He no longer wore the distinctive haircut, the tonsure. Instead, he grew vain about his dark hair, which he wore shoulder-length and carefully groomed. He kept his fingernails filed to perfection. He dressed like a dandy, in brightly colored jackets and caps — and he often wore armor, too, with a polished sword at his side.

Eagerly, he gave himself up to the delights of the rich and famous: music, dancing, gambling, and sex. He was a voracious reader of fiction, especially the knightly romances that were popular at the time. Spaniards were just then devouring the tales of *Amadis of Gaul*, which were Mediterranean adaptations of the legends of King Arthur and the knights of the Round Table. Though the romances were superficially Christian and favorable to virtues such as bravery and loyalty, they also tended to sentimentalize adultery and violence and to idealize the privileges of the noble classes.

These stories reinforced the worst tendencies in young Ignatius: his vanity, his promiscuity, and his violent temper — all of which he could justify in the name of honor, romance, and chivalry. He had many affairs, and he fought many duels.

Yet the romances also taught him some select virtues and a sort of piety. Before fighting duels, he always prayed to the Virgin Mary. And he once wrote a long poem in honor of St. Peter the Apostle, to whom Ignatius was especially devoted (perhaps because of the impetuous character they shared).

In 1517, Ignatius's patron, Don Velázquez, died, and the young man joined the army as a ranking officer. In battle, he showed himself to be brave and refined. He fought at the front lines, and in victory he never took booty from the defeated. In 1521, French military forces were advancing through Spain. When they were approaching Pamplona, Ignatius went to the city's defense with a small group of volunteers recruited from his hometown.

The French arrived with twelve thousand men and laid siege to the city. The people of Pamplona despaired, but Ignatius and his men fought on. They were ready to die. They made what they thought would be their last confessions to one another, since there was no priest nearby.

Finally, the French breached the wall and rushed into the city. Ignatius, about to attack, was suddenly struck by a cannonball, which passed through his legs, tearing open his left calf and breaking his right shin.

Even the victorious French must have admired his bravery. They dressed his wounds and sent him home to Loyola. There, however, the doctors found that his broken right leg had been set badly. The leg had to be rebroken and reset — and, later, a protruding end of bone had to be sawed off. All of these treatments caused the leg to be shortened, so that it later had to be stretched out by weights.

Keep in mind that all of this was carried out in the days before anesthesia and antisepsis. Ignatius, at age twenty-six, was suffering at an extremity of pain and with the constant danger of life-threatening infection. He took it all with gritted teeth and never uttered a cry; nor did he ask to be restrained with ropes, as surgical patients often were.

But the ordeal ground him down — and, for a while, he burned with fever and shook with pain, and it looked as if he would not survive. But on the eve of the feast of Sts. Peter and Paul, the fever broke, and he began to recover.

Still, he had a long convalescence ahead of him. He asked for his usual reading, the knightly romances, but there were none to be found. So he read what was at hand: a life of Christ and some biographies of the saints.

The saints aroused Ignatius's machismo. He longed to outdo them in fasting, vigils, and pilgrimages, as he had once longed to outdo Amadis and other knights in feats of arms. Indeed, he still fantasized about achieving glory as a knight, and he also dreamed of performing deeds that would impress a certain lady (whose name we do not know).

Soon, however, he noticed that his reveries of romance affected him in a way far different from his aspirations to holiness. The former left him feeling dissatisfied, whereas the latter gave him a sense of joy and peace. He realized, then, that the things of the world could never satisfy him, nor could the service of an earthly king or an earthly lady. He would give himself entirely to God.

As if to confirm this intuition, he was given a vision of the Blessed Virgin Mary and the child Jesus. After that, he would speak only of spiritual things. His family, knowing Ignatius's native rashness, feared for what he might do in his fervor. His brother Martin begged him not to embarrass the family.

Ignatius paid no heed. He set out immediately to outdo the saints. He made a pilgrimage to the sanctuary of Montserrat, where he spent three days preparing to make a good confession. He took off his rich clothes, gave them to the poor, and put on a garment of sackcloth. He hung his sword and dagger at the altar of the Virgin Mary, thus dedicating his knighthood to her cause. He remained in vigil until the following morning. Then he took to wandering, living off whatever he could beg, and sleeping in a cave.

He was happy. He had found peace, but it was to be short-lived. Soon he began to be haunted by his past sins and the thought that he had not confessed them well enough. These thoughts obsessed him so much that he contemplated suicide. But grace won through prayer, he soldiered on, and he recovered his peace.

The now-happy wanderer began to keep a notebook of his spiritual experiences. Over time, these accumulated notes would become the author's great classic, the *Spiritual Exercises*. He had a further opportunity to refine his teaching when he grew very ill and had to spend time in a public hospital. He taught his visitors and caretakers how to pray.

Once recovered, he set out on a pilgrimage to the Holy Land. Along the way, he suffered beatings, sickness, imprisonment, and shipwreck. After such an arduous journey, he arrived in the land of Jesus, only to face his most devastating disappointment. The friars charged with care of the holy sites ordered Ignatius to return home, as they were tired of finding ransoms for Christians imprisoned by the Muslims. He obeyed and returned to Spain early in 1524.

Back in Spain, Ignatius decided that, in order to serve others better, he must take up serious study of philosophy and theology. So he first entered Spanish universities and eventually found his way to Paris. He spent eleven years at this work — occasionally harassed by the Spanish Inquisition — and, in the end, he earned a master's degree, falling ill when he was just short of his doctorate.

Though just a student, he found himself regularly a master of disciples. Devout souls found Ignatius irresistibly attractive because he took them seriously and taught them a high standard for their lives. His first followers, however, did not persevere. Nor did the second group. It was the third group, which included Francis Xavier of Navarre, that would stay with Ignatius and share his way of life, by now embodied in the *Spiritual Exercises*.

The companions made their way to Italy, eventually, where they received permission to be ordained. Ignatius spent eighteen months preparing for his first Mass. Their immediate goal was to complete the pilgrimage to the Holy Land that Ignatius had left unfinished so many years before. On their return, at the end of one year, they would go to Rome and place themselves at the service of the Pope. Their pilgrimage, though, was not to be. Christians and Muslims were at war with one another, and safe passage to Jerusalem was practically impossible. So, at the end of the year, Ignatius and his companions went ahead with their plan to give themselves in service to the Pope.

Drawing from his military vocabulary, Ignatius called his brotherhood "The Company of Jesus." The official documents of their foundation, however, were drawn up by the authorities in Rome, who called Ignatius and his companions the "Society of Jesus." Soon, they became known more popularly as "the Jesuits."

The word *Jesuit* has a curious history. In Ignatius's time, it was a derogatory term used to describe someone who took the name of the Lord in vain, as in shouting "Jesus Christ!" as an exclamation of surprise, anger, or dismay. But the Society of Jesus earned this informal title because the holy name of Jesus was always on their lips, in their teaching and in prayer.

Ignatius's subsequent biography is identical with the Jesuits' history. The foundation of the order and its government were the substance of his work, and he managed it all prodigiously. He labored in a small office that served also as his bedroom. From 1524 to 1556 he wrote nearly seven thousand letters (that we know of).

And he didn't merely dash them off. He carefully crafted them, revised them, and rewrote them. He drafted the detailed legislation of his order and won papal approval for it. He oversaw the formation and ministry of the thousand men who joined the order during his lifetime — members who were soon at work in lands as far as India and China, Mexico and Ethiopia. He guided the development of dozens of schools (thirty-three by the end of his life), which, almost immediately, won the esteem that would ever be associated with the phrase "Jesuit education." As a spiritual director, he succeeded in remarkable ways. Many of his directees would one day be canonized or beatified: Francis Xavier, Peter Faber, Peter Canisius, and Francis Borgia.

In 1551, Ignatius submitted his resignation as father general of the Society of Jesus, hoping to return to more active ministry. But his brothers refused him that satisfaction. He continued as the order's superior to the very end of his life.

In the summer of 1556, he came down with a mild fever, which alarmed neither his brothers nor his doctors. But on July 30, 1556, Ignatius asked for the last sacraments. The next day he appeared so peaceful in prayer that no one noticed he was dying. He never received the anointing. The Church declared Ignatius "blessed" on July 27, 1609, and proclaimed him a saint on May 22, 1622.

The Spirit of Ignatius

More than for his many works, Ignatius has won renown for his particular spirit. It's a way of thinking about the world, and about other people, work, education, and priorities. Above all, it's a way of thinking about God and acting in relation to Him. It's a spirituality.

Ignatius was not a theologian or a systematic thinker. He wrote nothing anyone could call a treatise. But he lived and promoted a spirituality that was consistent, coherent, and distinctive in its emphases and methods.

In this he was like most of the great founders — like Mother Teresa of Calcutta in our own age. They seem never to tire of repeating a handful of aphorisms that sum up their most basic principles.

Ignatius's teaching found expression in several forms.

The best way to come to know Ignatius's spirituality is through his writings — his thousands of letters, his *Spiritual Exercises*, his autobiography, and the *Constitutions of the Society of Jesus*. On every page, Ignatius labored until he found the exact expression of his ideas. And these he conveyed in unornamented prose — spare, spartan, even military in its directness. His counsels are as basic and essential as the items in a soldier's rucksack.

We can also discover Ignatius's spirit in the life he lived, as it was witnessed, recorded, and imitated by his friends. His personal secretaries, for example, took care to mark down the table talk and office banter they had with the man they called "The Father" and "Our Father." They also left vivid descriptions of his manners, his habits, and his works.

The interpretation of Ignatius's words and life has continued on through future generations of his spiritual family. Jesuit authors have written countless biographies, commentaries, poems, short stories, and even psychoanalyses reflecting on the life and work of their spiritual father.

Certain themes arise again and again in the works of Ignatius and his commentators:

1. **"Seek God in all things."** The phrase recurs in Ignatius's works. Ignatius's way was unlike many other forms of religious life. He asked his followers not to remove themselves from the world, but to work within the world and its institutions. They would find God there, amid "all things," because He has created all things. Moreover, in baptism, God made us His children and His heirs, and so we share with Him in the government of all creation. Ignatius marveled over this in a letter to young students in Portugal: "For [God] has placed under our ministry, not only all that is under heaven but even the whole of His sublime court, not excepting even any of the heavenly hierarchy." This rule over creation — our small corner of it — is what we exercise in our everyday work.

2. **"For the greater glory of God."** This was Ignatius's motto. He taught that it is important for us not just to do good things, but to do them for the right reasons. For it is certainly possible to perform seemingly good work for bad reasons: merely for money or fame, or to draw attention to ourselves, or to draw attention away from others, or to put off doing the less glamorous work we really should be doing. If we offer every task "for the greater glory of God," as Ignatius did, we will begin with the only worthy end in mind. If we work for any lesser goal, we will never find peace or satisfaction in what we do.

3. **Service.** Ignatius hated selfishness. He called it "self-love," and he set it in opposition to true charity

toward oneself. If we really want what is best for our-selves, we will work for the good of others. For self-love is the root cause of much sadness and dissatisfaction. Ignatius urged his followers to find the divine image in all people — even difficult people and sinners — just as they were to find God in all things. Ignatian spirituality leads us to care for the comfort of others rather than our own comfort, to care for the salvation of others as a means to our own salvation. This concern would drive us constantly to work for the good of friends, family, and co-workers: to correct them when they are in error; to exhort them when they are living in sin; to teach them when they are living in ignorance; to feed and clothe them when they are in want.

4. **Detachment.** Because Ignatius saw the goodness in creation, he also saw how easily our love for things can become disordered. We are always tempted to place our own comfort and pleasure above our desire to do God's will. We become attached to the things that bring us comfort or pleasure, and soon we are willing to neglect our duty or commit sin in order to get them or keep them. Thus, we must detach ourselves from the things of the world. We must practice self-denial and learn to discipline our cravings. We must love our friends, our family, our food, and our work *for God's sake*, and not merely for our own satisfaction. For the things of this world pass away, and none can satisfy us for very long. Only God will do.

5. **Obedience.** As a knight and a military officer, Ignatius knew that people cannot live without hierarchy of authority. But this is always a hierarchy of service, the higher serving the lower. No enterprise can endure disobedience. That's why Ignatius required an extreme

sort of obedience. He even went so far as to call it "the obedience of a corpse," for a corpse can put up no resistance. Ignatius insisted that everyone owes total obedience to the Church and its teaching authority, especially as it is embodied in the Pope, because this authority came from Christ Himself. Our saint never said this would be easy. It would require humility, trust in God's will, and a deep knowledge of oneself as a sinner, untrustworthy in all things.

6. **Method.** Ignatius counseled people not to become overly preoccupied with methods of prayer, but rather to "do what you can calmly and gently." Still, he found certain practices helpful:

- A deep devotion to Jesus and a love for His holy name.
- A personal encounter with Jesus in the Gospels. Ignatius urged people to meditate upon the Gospel scenes, to "see the place," to use their imagination to enter the story as one of the participants, to become more than a reader of God's saving works, more than a witness — to become a friend and a beloved of Jesus Christ.
- Knowledge of oneself. Ignatius taught his followers how to examine their conscience thoroughly every day. He wrote the *Spiritual Exercises* as a thoroughgoing examination of oneself that could be renewed at regular intervals.
- A spiritual retreat. The *Spiritual Exercises* were intended to be undergone during a prolonged period of silent study and prayer. Ignatius prescribed a yearly retreat for those who were serious about the spiritual life.

Ignatius's way was not monastic. He mapped it out for people like himself, knights-errant in the spiritual life, who would journey into the world to accomplish great things for the sake of God's glory and the honor of the Blessed Virgin Mary. Thus, his method of prayer emphasized the things of the world in ways that his predecessors had not. He also warned that the consolations of such a life would be far different from those of a hermit or a monk, whose "fixed, immobile attention" to heavenly matters "is repugnant to our state" as pilgrims in the world.

Ignatian prayer, then, is contemplative. It meditates upon things. It engages the imagination and the intellect. But it does not stop there. Prayer, according to Ignatius, should be productive of activity. It should fuel the impulse to serve. It should make the mind and heart ready, willing, and able to serve. Prayer leads to action, which, in turn, leads us back to prayer.

Ignatius's secretary, Father Jerome Nadal, wrote:

> This is what I would like to call the circle of occupations. . . . If you are occupied with your neighbor and with the service of God . . . in any office, God will help you afterwards more efficaciously in your prayer. And this more effective divine aid will in turn enable you to take care of your neighbor with more courage and spiritual profit.

According to Father Nadal, this "circle of occupations" defined the life of Ignatius, who was a "contemplative even while engaged in action."

Work does not distract us from prayer; nor does prayer distract us from work. If we live and pray for God's glory, then everything we do is a prayer. Our work is a collaboration in God's providence, a working-out of His plan for our corner of creation and our moment in history.

We live in an odd time, when both workaholism and work-evasion are epidemic in our offices, assembly lines, and shop floors. Philosophers and consultants present us with one "work ethic" after another, and each theoretical house-of-cards stands for a day as a fad that consumes the international business world. And the fads play themselves out in seminars and motivational posters until, one day, a strong economic, social, or political wind comes to knock it all down.

Ignatius knew — and we must learn — that what the workplace needs is not another theory, not another system, but the living presence of Jesus. Over the course of a career and a lifetime, that's the only thing that works.

Ignatian texts used in this book have been adapted from the following sources:

Letters   *Letters of St. Ignatius of Loyola*, selected and translated by William J. Young, S.J. (Chicago: Loyola University Press, 1959).

Autobiography   *St. Ignatius' Own Story*, translated by William J. Young, S.J. (Chicago: Loyola University Press, 1998).

Exercises   *The Spiritual Exercises of St. Ignatius*, translated by Louis J. Puhl, S.J. (Chicago: Loyola University Press, 1951).

Constitutions   *The Constitutions of the Society of Jesus*, translated by George E. Ganss, S.J. (St. Louis, Mo.: Institute of Jesuit Sources, 1970).

Pilgrim   *Ignatius of Loyola: The Pilgrim Saint*, by José Ignacio Tellechea Idígoras, translated by Michael Buckley, S.J. (Chicago: Loyola University Press, 1994).

Modern   *A Modern Scriptural Approach to the Spiritual Exercises*, by David M. Stanley, S.J. (Chicago: Loyola University Press, 1967).

Psychology   *Ignatius of Loyola: The Psychology of a Saint*, by W.W. Meissner, S.J., M.D.

| | (New Haven, Conn.: Yale University Press, 1992). |
| *Woodstock* | Website of Woodstock Theological Center: Writings of St. Ignatius of Loyola and St. Claude la Colombière: www.georgetown.edu/centers/woodstock/ignatius/Jesuit_texts.htm |

Note: The *Catechism of the Catholic Church* cites Ignatius's *Spiritual Exercises* three times. Whenever quoting these passages, we have used the texts from the *Catechism*, which would be more familiar to the average Catholic.

1. The World Needs You

Ignatius impressed upon young students the urgency of their mission — how rare Christian witness was in the world, how desperately the world needed them. Do his words ring less true today? Doesn't today's world need you even more?

If you recognize this obligation and wish to employ yourselves in promoting God's honor, the times you are living in make it incumbent indeed on you to make your desire known by works.

Can you find a place where the Divine Majesty is in honor today, or where His infinite greatness is worshiped, where His wisdom and infinite goodness are known, or His most holy will obeyed?

Behold, rather, with deep grief, how His holy name is everywhere ignored, despised, blasphemed. The teaching of Jesus Christ is cast off, His example forgotten, and the price of His blood lost in a certain sense, as far as we are concerned, because there are so few to profit by it.

Behold likewise your neighbors, images of the Most Holy Trinity and capable of enjoying His glory Whom all the world serves, members of Christ, redeemed by so much pain, opprobrium, and blood. Behold, I say, the miseries that surround them, the darkness of ignorance that envelopes them, and the whirlwind of desires, empty fears, and other passions that torment them, set upon by so many visible and invisible enemies, with the peril of losing, I do not say their property or their earthly lives, but an eternal kingdom and its happiness by falling into the insufferable misfortune of everlasting fire.

Letters 125-126

- If I wish God to be glorified, I must make that desire known by works.
- God has called me to share in His rule over all the earth.
- What can I do to set my neighbors free from the miserable whirlwind of desires, empty fears, and other passions that torment them?

As he went ashore, he saw a great crowd; and he had compassion for them, because they were like sheep without a shepherd; and he began to teach them many things.   MARK 6:34

Behold your neighbors, images of the Most Holy Trinity and capable of enjoying His glory. Behold members of Christ, redeemed by so much pain, abuse, and blood. Behold the miseries that surround them.

2. Use the Gifts God Gave You

God is all-powerful, and He has given us His own life in baptism. He has called us to be perfect, and He will give us the graces to answer that call. In the following letter, Ignatius "put the spurs" to eighty young students in Coimbra, Portugal, urging them to be worthy vessels of God's grace as they carried out their daily work.

Our Lord Jesus Christ . . . tells us, "Be perfect, therefore, as your heavenly Father is perfect" (Matthew 5:48). It is certain, then, that for His part He is ready, on condition that we have a vessel of humility and desire to receive His graces, and that He sees that we make good use of the gifts we have received and cooperate diligently and earnestly with His grace.

On this point I will not fail to put the spurs even to those of you who are running so willingly. For I can tell you that you must be persistent both in your studies and in the practice of virtue if you are to come up to the expectations which so many entertain of you. There are persons, not only in the kingdom of Portugal but in many other countries, who — considering the helps and advantages of every kind, both interior and exterior, that God gives you — rightly hope for more than ordinary results in you.

Letters 121-122

■ Jesus is ready to give His grace, if I am ready to receive it.
■ Have I made good use of the gifts He has already given me?
■ Do I live the life that people expect of a Christian who has had so many advantages?

From his fullness we have all received, grace upon grace.   JOHN 1:16

Jesus is ready to give, on condition that I am a vessel of humility and desire.

3. Prayer for Generosity

God will not be outdone in generosity. He has given us everything we have in life, save our sins. For the sake of our salvation, He gave His only Son. His self-giving is nowhere so evident as in the Mass, where Christ gives us everything He has: body, blood, soul, and divinity. God has held nothing back. To imitate Him, we must give as He gives. Ignatius taught his Company to pray this prayer to obtain a divine spirit of generosity.

Teach us, good Lord, to serve You as You deserve,
to give and not count the cost,
to fight and not to heed the wounds,
to toil and not to seek for rest,
to labor and not ask for any reward
except that of knowing that we do Your will.

THINK ABOUT IT

- May I never count the cost of my devotion to Jesus. He gave His all for me.
- May I grow in the virtues of generosity, fortitude, and perseverance.
- May I seek God's will, know God's will, do God's will.

JUST IMAGINE

"Give, and it will be given to you. A good measure, pressed down, shaken together, running over, will be put into your lap; for the measure you give will be the measure you get back."   LUKE 6:38

Teach us, good Lord, to give and not count the cost.

4. Higher Goals, Better Striving

If we are working each day for God's glory, we should work harder and with greater care than those who are working merely for money or human ambition.

For his encouragement each one should keep before his eyes, not those who he thinks will accomplish less, but rather those who are active and energetic. Do not ever permit the children of this world to show greater care and solicitude for the things of time than you show for those of eternity. It should bring a blush to your cheek to see them run to death more unhesitatingly than you to life. Hold yourselves as little worth if a courtier serve with greater care merely to have the favor of an earthly prince than you do for the favor of the King of Heaven, and if a soldier for the honor and glory of a victory and a little booty gets himself ready and battles more bravely than you do for the victory and triumph over the world, the devil, and yourselves, with the kingdom of heaven and everlasting glory as your prize.

Letters 123

THINK ABOUT IT

- I will imitate the work of the best, and I will offer my work to God.
- I will strive to do better for heavenly goals than others do for earthly rewards.

■ I work to conquer the world, the devil, and myself. The kingdom of heaven and everlasting glory are my prize.

Do you not know that in a race the runners all compete, but only one receives the prize? Run in such a way that you may win it. Athletes exercise self-control in all things; they do it to receive a perishable wreath, but we an imperishable one.

1 CORINTHIANS 9:24-25

Do not permit the children of this world to show greater care for the things of time than you show for those of eternity.

5. Work: A Continuous Prayer

Our prayer is not limited to the time we spend reciting devotions, or meditating, or in active conversation with God. Ignatius taught students that all their everyday life can be a prayer, if they make prayer their sincere desire.

The demands of your life of study do not permit you to devote much time to prayer, yet you can make up for this by desires, since the time you devote to your various exercises is a continuous prayer, seeing that you are engaged in them only for God's service.

Letters 129

THINK ABOUT IT

- I must pray as much as I really can, and not be anxious about what I cannot do.
- I must make up for any lack of prayer by my desire to pray.
- I must purify my motives so that I work only for God's service.

JUST IMAGINE

Whether you eat or drink, or whatever you do, do everything for the glory of God.   1 CORINTHIANS 10:31

REMEMBER

The time you devote to your work can be a continuous prayer.

6. Keep the Goal in Mind

It is easy for us to get so wrapped up in what we're doing that we forget why we're doing it. Ignatius urges us to "seek God in all things." The following counsel is adapted from Ignatius's Constitutions of the Society of Jesus, *n. 288.*

Make diligent efforts to keep your intention right in all particular details. Always aim at serving and pleasing the Divine Goodness for its own sake and because of the incomparable love and benefits with which God has anticipated us, rather than for fear of punishments or hope of rewards, although you ought to draw help also from these. Seek God our Lord in all things, stripping off from yourself the love of creatures to the extent that this is possible, in order to turn your love upon your Creator, by loving Him in all creatures and all of them in Him, in conformity with His holy and divine will.

THINK ABOUT IT

■ I must make a diligent effort to have good intentions in all my work.
■ Every detail matters.
■ Pleasing God is the goal — more important than worldly success.

JUST IMAGINE

Whatever your task, put yourselves into it, as done for the Lord and not for your masters, since you know that from the Lord you will receive the inheritance as your reward; you serve the Lord Christ.

COLOSSIANS 3:23-24

REMEMBER

Seek God our Lord in all things.

7. God Is Here

Father Antonio Brandão, a Portuguese Jesuit, submitted to Ignatius a list of fifteen questions on the spiritual life. The sixth question asked what method of meditation was best. Ignatius recommended the constant practice of the presence of God.

They should practice the seeking of God's presence in all things, in their conversations, their walks, in all that they see, taste, hear, understand, in all their actions, since His Divine Majesty is truly in all things by His presence, power, and essence. This kind of meditation which finds God our Lord in all things is easier than raising oneself to the consideration of divine truths which are more abstract and which demand something of an effort if we are to keep our attention on them. But this method is an excellent exercise to prepare us for great visitations of our Lord, even in prayers that are rather short.

Letters 240

THINK ABOUT IT

- I should practice the seeking of God's presence in all my actions.
- Finding God in all things is easier than the methods that seem more impressive.
- I should regularly remind myself of God's presence by saying short, silent prayers — even just the name of Jesus.

JUST IMAGINE

And Jesus came and said to them, ". . . Remember, I am with you always, to the end of the age."

MATTHEW 28:18, 20

REMEMBER

His Divine Majesty is truly in all things by His presence, power, and essence.

When the Pope sent Jesuits on diplomatic missions, Ignatius advised them to deal with different people in different ways, to please them whenever possible, but to please God first.

In dealing with people of position or influence, if you are to win their affection for the greater glory of God our Lord, look first to their disposition and accommodate yourselves to them. If they are of a lively temper, quick and merry of speech, follow their lead in your dealings with them when you talk of good and holy things, and do not be too serious, glum, and reserved. If they are shy and retiring, slow to speak, serious and weighty in their talk, use the same manner with them, because such ways will be gratifying to them. "I have become all things to all people" (1 Corinthians 9:22). Do not forget that, if one is of a lively disposition and deals with another who is like him, there is very great danger of their failing to come to an agreement if they are not of one spirit. And therefore, if one knows that one is of such a lively disposition, he ought to approach another of similar traits well prepared by self-examination and determined to be patient and not to get out of sorts with him, especially if he knows him to be in poor health. If he is dealing with one of slower temper, there is not so much danger of a disagreement arising from words hastily spoken. *Letters 51*

- Looking first to the disposition of others, I should accommodate myself to them.
- Before approaching my colleagues, I should be well prepared, examining my motives and my disposition.
- I must decide to be patient and not to get out of sorts.

JUST IMAGINE

To the weak I became weak, so that I might win the weak. I have become all things to all people, that I might by all means save some. I do it all for the sake of the gospel, so that I may share in its blessings.

1 CORINTHIANS 9:22-23

REMEMBER

Win the affection of others for the greater glory of God.

9. Don't Procrastinate

The Pope had chosen two Jesuits, Fathers Salmeron and Broet, to represent him in Ireland. Ignatius urged them not to put off work that is unpleasant or difficult.

In business matters be generous with your time; that is, if you can, do today what you promise for tomorrow.

Letters 52

THINK ABOUT IT

- I must be generous with my time and not hoard it to myself.
- I must plan my workday based on the needs of others and the tasks at hand — not according to my pleasures and my peeves.
- Do I turn promptly to the work that needs to be done, even if I find it dull?
- Can people depend on me to complete my work on time?

JUST IMAGINE

[To one man, Jesus said:] "Follow me." But he said, "Lord, first let me go and bury my father." But Jesus said to him, "Let the dead bury their own dead; but as for you, go and proclaim the kingdom of God." Another said, "I will follow you, Lord; but let me first say farewell to those at my home." Jesus said to him, "No one who puts a hand to the plow and looks back is fit for the kingdom of God."   LUKE 9:59-62

REMEMBER

If possible, do today what you promise for tomorrow.

10. Extra Effort

The Jesuits in Coimbra, Portugal, had established many vibrant apostolates. St. Ignatius warned them against complacency, and he urged them not to let their efforts slacken. He emphasized the necessity of intellectual as well as spiritual formation.

For the love of God, do not be careless or tepid. For if tautness breaks the bow, idleness breaks the soul; while on the contrary, according to Solomon, the soul of those who work shall be made fat [see Proverbs 13:4]. Try to maintain a holy and discreet ardor in work and in the pursuit of learning as well as of virtue. With one as with the other, one energetic act is worth a thousand that are listless, and what a lazy man cannot accomplish in many years an energetic man usually achieves in a short time.　*Letters 123*

THINK ABOUT IT

- Idleness breaks the soul.
- I should try to maintain a holy and discreet ardor in work.
- I must never stop learning or actively pursuing virtue.

JUST IMAGINE

"And about five o'clock he went out and found others standing around; and he said to them, 'Why are you standing here idle all day?'"　MATTHEW 20:6

One energetic act is worth a thousand that are listless; and what a lazy man cannot accomplish in many years an energetic man usually achieves in a short time.

11. Modesty in All Things

In all our actions — our words, our gestures, our posture — we should communicate the respect we have for others. The following counsel is adapted from Ignatius's Constitutions of the Society of Jesus, *n. 250.*

Preserve yourself in peace and true humility of soul, keeping silence when silence should be kept and, when you must speak, speaking with discretion. May your peace and humility show in the modesty of your countenance, the maturity of your walk, and in all your movements, without showing any sign of impatience or pride. In everything, try and desire to give the advantage to others, esteeming them all in their hearts as better than yourself (Philippians 2:3). Show outward respect befitting each one's state. In this way, you will grow in devotion and praise for God our Lord, Whose image each one should try to recognize in his neighbor.

THINK ABOUT IT

- Do I try to find God's image in all my colleagues, customers, employees, and superiors?
- Do others know that I respect them, regardless of our differences?
- Do my words or facial expressions convey impatience or excessive pride?

Do nothing from selfish ambition or conceit, but in humility regard others as better than yourselves. Let each of you look not to your own interests, but to the interests of others. Let the same mind be in you that was in Christ Jesus,

> who, though he was in the form of God,
>> did not regard equality with God
>> as something to be exploited,
> but emptied himself,
>> taking the form of a slave,
>> being born in human likeness.

PHILIPPIANS 2:3-7

REMEMBER

In everything, try and desire to give the advantage to others, esteeming them all in their hearts as better than yourself.

12. Speak Moderately and Politely

Here is further advice to Fathers Salmeron and Broet, on "How to negotiate and deal with others in our Lord."

In your dealings with all, be slow to speak and say little, especially with your equals or subordinates. Be ready to listen for long periods and until each has had his say. Answer the questions put to you, come to an end, and take your leave. If a rejoinder is offered, let your reply be as brief as possible, and take leave promptly and politely.

Letters 51

THINK ABOUT IT

- If I am slow to speak, I will be better able to listen to others.
- I should let others have their say and try not to cut them short.
- I should give direct answers, without excuses or evasions, to the questions others ask me.
- I should not let idle talk waste my time or the time of my co-workers. We owe our employer the hours for which we are paid.

JUST IMAGINE

[Jesus said:] "Let anyone with ears listen! But to what will I compare this generation? It is like children sitting in the marketplaces and calling to one another,

'We played the flute for you, and you did not
     dance;
we wailed, and you did not mourn.' "

MATTHEW 11:15-17

REMEMBER

Be slow to speak and say little. Be ready to listen until
all have had their say.

13. The Benefit of the Doubt

*Charity is a state of mind before it shows itself in deeds.
We should never make rash judgments of other people. The
following gem is one of three quotations of St. Ignatius
included in the* Catechism of the Catholic Church *(n.
2478).*

Every good Christian ought to be more ready to give
a favorable interpretation to another's statement
than to condemn it. But if he cannot do so, let him
ask how the other understands it. And if the latter
understands it badly, let the former correct him with
love. If that does not suffice, let the Christian try all
suitable ways to bring the other to a correct interpretation
so that he may be saved.

Exercises, n. 22

THINK ABOUT IT

- Do I assume the good intentions of others, even
  when I disagree with them?
- Do I try to understand the point of view of those
  who disagree with me?
- When others are mistaken, I should correct them
  with love.

JUST IMAGINE

"But I say to you that if you are angry with a brother
or sister, you will be liable to judgment; and if you
insult a brother or sister, you will be liable to the

council; and if you say, 'You fool,' you will be liable
to the hell of fire."   MATTHEW 5:22

REMEMBER

Every good Christian ought to be more ready to give
a favorable interpretation to another's statement than
to condemn it.

14. Correcting Others

Ignatius urged his companions to correct one another's faults. Such "fraternal correction" is an invaluable act of charity. This is how friends help friends advance toward perfection.

[We turn now to] the correction of another. For this to be successful it will help much if the corrector has some authority, or acts with great affection, an affection that can be recognized. If either of these qualities is absent, the correction will fail — that is, there will be no amendment. For this reason it would not be proper for everybody to undertake such correction. But in whatever manner it is done, and if one is reasonably certain that it will be well taken, one's admonition should not be too forthright, but toned down and presented without offense; because one sin leads to another, and it is quite possible that once committed, it will not dispose the sinner to accept even a well-intentioned correction in the right spirit.

Letters 242

THINK ABOUT IT

■ I should gently help others to see and correct their faults.

■ I should make corrections only when I know what I'm talking about, and when I can do so with genuine affection.

■ I should pray before I point out the faults of another.

"If another member of the church sins against you, go and point out the fault when the two of you are alone. If the member listens to you, you have regained that one. But if you are not listened to, take one or two others along with you, so that every word may be confirmed by the evidence of two or three witnesses. If the member refuses to listen to them, tell it to the church; and if the offender refuses to listen even to the church, let such a one be to you as a Gentile and a tax collector."   MATTHEW 18:15-17

REMEMBER

If we make corrections that lack authority or affection, our corrections will fail; there will be no amendment.

15. Instructions on Dealing With Others

Ignatius gave the following points of advice, early in 1546, to the Jesuit priests serving as advisers at the Council of Trent, a difficult assignment.

Be slow to speak. Be considerate and kindly, especially when it comes to defining matters which are being discussed or likely to be discussed in the council.

Be slow to speak, and only after having first listened quietly, so that you may understand the meaning, leanings, and desires of those who speak. You will thus know better when to speak and when to be silent.

When such matters are being discussed, I should rather consider the reasons on both sides without showing any attachment to my own opinion, and try to avoid causing dissatisfaction to anyone.

Letters 94

THINK ABOUT IT

- I should not be dogmatic about matters that are not dogmas.
- I should try to respect my co-workers and understand their opinions.
- I should carefully listen to both sides of any dispute.

Honor everyone. Love the family of believers.

1 PETER 2:17

Be slow to speak, and only after having first listened quietly so that you may understand the meaning, leanings, and desires of those who speak.

16. Learn to Listen

One of Ignatius's secretaries, Father Gonçalves da Câmara, recalled how Ignatius would conduct himself in conversation.

When the Father [Ignatius] began speaking with someone, at first he would let the man speak as much as he wanted, and then he would speak to him in such a way that, even if the person were very imperfect, he would not be scandalized. When he would get to know the person better and the person felt more at ease, the Father would slowly proceed and, without any violence, change the whole game.

Pilgrim 574

THINK ABOUT IT

- I should try to let others speak as much as they want, before I begin to speak myself.
- I should try to listen to what others say to me, on the phone or face-to-face.
- I should try not to treat the concerns of others as distractions or interruptions.

JUST IMAGINE

The Lord's servant must not be quarrelsome but kindly to everyone, an apt teacher, patient, correcting opponents with gentleness.   2 TIMOTHY 2:24-25

When Ignatius began speaking with someone, he would first let the man speak as much as he wanted.

17. On Flatterers and Friends

Francis Jimenez de Miranda was a powerful man who was living a sinful life. He was surrounded by many hangers-on and yes-men who encouraged him in his ways. Yet he was impressed by Ignatius and wanted to make up for his sins by founding a college and entrusting it to the Jesuits. Ignatius cared little for the man's offer of money, but much for his soul. Ignatius visited him and wrote him letters urging him first to repent. The man clung to his ways. So Ignatius wrote him a long, bracing letter, from which the following is taken.

This is no time for pretenses with those who love you. Do not look upon him as a friend or servant, but as a mortal enemy of your soul, who attends you with flattery, especially those who reassure you and hold you in your sins. What you need is penance and much of it.

This means that you must not only withdraw from your sin and be sorry for it, but that you must make satisfaction for past sins, and unburden your conscience of so much.

Letters 397

THINK ABOUT IT

- I should favor truth-tellers over those who flatter me.
- I will avoid paying excessive or insincere compliments.

■ I will be frank in confronting those who persist in serious sin.

Then the Pharisees went and plotted to entrap [Jesus] in what he said. So they sent their disciples to him, along with the Herodians, saying, "Teacher, we know that you are sincere, and teach the way of God in accordance with truth, and show deference to no one; for you do not regard people with partiality. Tell us, then, what you think. Is it lawful to pay taxes to the emperor, or not?" But Jesus, aware of their malice, said, "Why are you putting me to the test, you hypocrites?"   MATTHEW 22:15-18

REMEMBER

Do not look upon him as a friend, but as a mortal enemy of your soul, who attends you with flattery, especially those who reassure you in your sins.

18. Work for Peace

The heart is restless until it rests in God. But that rest follows after the hard work of growing in virtue and conquering vice. For it is sin that makes us unhappy and ill at ease.

Experience proves that in this life peace and satisfaction are had, not by the listless, but by those who are fervent in God's service. And rightly so. For in the effort they make to overcome themselves and to rid themselves of self-love, they rid themselves of the roots of all passion and unrest. And with the acquirement of habits of virtue they naturally succeed in acting easily and cheerfully in accordance with these virtues.

By this means they dispose themselves to receive holy consolations from God our faithful consoler, for "To everyone who conquers I will give some of the hidden manna" (Revelation 2:17).

Letters 122

THINK ABOUT IT

- Lazy people do not know peace in this life.
- If I rid myself of self-love, I will root out all unrest from my soul.
- As I grow in virtue, I will more easily and happily fulfill the will of God.
- God will console me and give me peace.

"Peace I leave with you; my peace I give to you. I do not give to you as the world gives. Do not let your hearts be troubled, and do not let them be afraid."

JOHN 14:27

REMEMBER

In this life, peace and satisfaction belong not to the listless, but to those who are fervent in God's service.

Hours of study are never wasted. They are an offering to God and an inspiration to our neighbor. The following is condensed from Ignatius's advice to students in Portugal.

Do not imagine that in this time given to your studies you are of no use to your neighbor; because, besides the profit to yourself which well-ordered charity requires — "Have pity on your own soul, pleasing God" [Sirach 30:24, in the Latin Vulgate Bible] — you are serving God's honor and glory in many ways.

First, by your present labor and the intention with which you undertake and regulate everything for your neighbor's edification, just as soldiers waiting to get supplies of arms and munitions for the operation about to be launched cannot say that their labor is not in the service of their king. Even if death should overtake one before he begins to work exteriorly for his neighbor, he shall not for that reason have failed in the service of his neighbor. He will have helped him by the mere fact of his preparation. But besides the intention for the future, he should each day offer himself to God for his neighbor. As God is willing to accept the offering, he can serve as an instrument for the help of his neighbor no less than he would have done by preaching or hearing confessions.

The second way is to attain a high degree of virtue, because you will thus be able to make your neighbor as you are yourselves. For it is God's will that the process of reproduction observed in material things be observed in spiritual things. In the generation of man or animals, a cause or agent of the same species is required — something that possesses the same form as the thing that is to be transmitted. In a similar way, to transmit the form of humility, patience, charity, and so forth, God wills that the immediate cause He uses as instrument — such as the preacher or confessor — be humble, charitable, patient. When you benefit yourselves with growth in virtue, you are also of great service to the neighbor. You are preparing an instrument that is not less, but better, fitted to confer grace by leading a virtuous life than by leading a learned one, although both learning and virtue are required if the instrument is to be perfect. *Letters 128-129*

THINK ABOUT IT

- Charity requires me to care for myself.
- When I study, I am preparing to serve others more effectively in the future.
- In order to reproduce the Christian life in others, I must first have it myself.

JUST IMAGINE

Blessed is the one who reads ..., and blessed are those who hear and who keep what is written.

REVELATION 1:3

REMEMBER

Both learning and virtue are required if the instrument is to be perfect.

Ignatius points out the proper order of means and ends.

In every good choice . . . , our intention must be simple. I must consider only the end for which I am created — that is, for the praise of God our Lord and for the salvation of my soul: Hence, whatever I choose must help me to this end for which I am created.

I must not subject and fit the end to the means, but the means to the end. Many first choose marriage, which is a means, and secondarily the service of God our Lord in marriage, though the service of God is the end. So also others first choose to have good jobs, and afterwards to serve God in them. Such persons do not go directly to God, but want God to conform wholly to their disordered attachments. Consequently, they make of the end a means, and of the means an end. As a result, what they ought to seek first, they seek last.

Therefore, my first aim should be to seek to serve God, which is the end, and only after that, if it is more profitable, to have a good job or marry, for these are means to the end. Nothing must move me to use such means, or to deprive myself of them, save only the service and praise of God our Lord, and the salvation of my soul.

Exercises, n. 169

- In all my choices, I must first try to acquire the right intention, the right desire, the right goal.
- Do secondary matters get first priority in my thoughts and my prayers?
- I must resolve to seek God's will — and not to wish for God to do my will.

JUST IMAGINE

"Therefore do not worry, saying, 'What will we eat?' or 'What will we drink?' or 'What will we wear?' For it is the Gentiles who strive for all these things; and indeed your heavenly Father knows that you need all these things. But strive first for the kingdom of God and his righteousness, and all these things will be given to you as well."   MATTHEW 6:31-33

REMEMBER

My first aim should be to serve God, which is the end, and only after that, if it is more profitable, to have a good job or marry, for these are means to the end.

21. Decision Making

One of Ignatius's secretaries, Father Gonçalves da Câmara, recalled his management style and method of making decisions.

Our Father [Ignatius] is accustomed to being so firm in things which he undertakes, that this steadfastness amazes everyone. Here are the reasons that come to my mind. First is that he carefully considers each matter before deciding it. Second, he prays very much on this subject and is illuminated by God. Third, he makes no particular decision without hearing the opinion of those who are competent in the matter, and he asks them for the majority of the circumstances, with the sole exception of those of which he has full cognizance. He was accustomed also, very often, when he did not have full knowledge of the matter, to postpone it and to let some general opinions on the topic suffice for the moment.

Psychology 204

THINK ABOUT IT

- I should make informed and careful decisions.
- I should pray before making any important decisions.
- I should not rush into a decision when I really should learn more about the matter and a resolution is not urgently needed.

The apostles and the elders met together to consider this matter. After there had been much debate, Peter stood up.... The whole assembly kept silence, and listened....   ACTS 15:6-7, 12

I should pray about a subject and make no particular decision without hearing the opinion of those who are competent in the matter.

22. On Time

Most people who succeed are faithful to a schedule. They keep their appointments. Ignatius's secretaries recalled that he was steadfast in this, even amid circumstances that could have excused his delay or absence.

In November of the year 1552, Ignatius set out on a journey. . . . On the morning of the day fixed for their departure, it was raining in torrents. Father Polanco said to Ignatius that it would perhaps be more advisable to put off their departure till the morrow, so that he might not come to harm because of the pouring rain. But our Father answered: "We leave at once. For thirty years I have never let myself be put off by rain or wind, or by any inclemency of the weather, from beginning punctually at the appointed time any work in the service of God our Lord." So they set out at the hour appointed.

Psychology 188-189

THINK ABOUT IT

- I must not look for excuses to get out of work.
- I should keep appointments because others are depending on me.
- I should respect deadlines, budgets, and other constraints imposed on my work.

At that very hour some Pharisees came and said to [Jesus], "Get away from here, for Herod wants to kill you." He said to them, "Go and tell that fox for me, 'Listen, I am casting out demons and performing cures today and tomorrow, and on the third day I finish my work.' "   LUKE 13:31-32

I should never let myself be put off by rain or wind, or by any inclemency of the weather, from beginning punctually at the appointed time any work in the service of God our Lord.

23. Making Sacrifices for Others

The following story, adapted from an account by Father Pedro de Ribadeneira, Ignatius's secretary, shows how far Ignatius would go to comfort friends who were suffering.

Ignatius once paid a visit to a former disciple who was very sick and depressed. Out of great charity, Ignatius asked if there was anything he could do to bring happiness into his life and dispel the gloom and sadness he was experiencing. After thinking about it for some time, the sick man said something quite silly: "If you could sing a little and dance a little as they do in your country, in Vizcaya, I think this could give me some consolation."

Ignatius replied: "Would that make you happy?"

"Oh, yes, very happy," said the sick man.

Ignatius's charity prevailed over his own personal preference and restraint; he figured such a request could only come from a very sick man indeed, and so he did what the sick man asked him to do. When he had finished, he said: "Please do not ask me to do that again, because I shall not do it." The sick man was so overjoyed by Ignatius's charity that after he left, the depression that was eating up the sick man's heart was lifted; he began to improve, and after a few days, he was cured.

Pilgrim 297-298

- I should smile, for the sake of others, when I would rather not smile.
- I should not avoid speaking to people I find dull or annoying.
- The saints, including Ignatius and especially the Blessed Virgin Mary, will go far to help me when I am suffering.

JUST IMAGINE

There was a wedding in Cana of Galilee, and the mother of Jesus was there.... When the wine gave out, the mother of Jesus said to him, "They have no wine." And Jesus said to her, "Woman, what concern is that to you and to me? My hour has not yet come." His mother said to the servants, "Do whatever he tells you." ... Jesus said to them, "Fill the jars with water.... Now draw some out, and take it to the chief steward." So they took it. When the steward tasted the water that had become wine..., the steward called the bridegroom and said to him, "Everyone serves the good wine first, and then the inferior wine after the guests have become drunk. But you have kept the good wine until now." JOHN 2:1, 3-5, 7-10

REMEMBER

Ignatius's charity prevailed over his own personal preference and restraint.

24. Speaking of Co-workers

If we have nothing good to say about our colleagues, we should say nothing. Otherwise, we risk lying or damaging someone's reputation.

Nothing should be said to lessen the good name of others, or to complain about them. For if I reveal a hidden mortal sin of another, I sin mortally; if I reveal a hidden venial sin, I sin venially; if I reveal a defect, I manifest my own.   *Exercises*, n. 41

THINK ABOUT IT

- I should always speak well of others, even of those who oppose me.
- Do I — by my consent, my smiles, or my willingness to listen — encourage others to criticize their friends and colleagues?
- When I am tempted to point out the fault of another, I will consider whether I might have that fault or a similar fault.

JUST IMAGINE

"Do not judge, and you will not be judged; do not condemn, and you will not be condemned. Forgive, and you will be forgiven."   Luke 6:37

REMEMBER

If I reveal the defect of another, I manifest my own.

When we strive to follow Jesus, we will face misunder-
standing. This is especially true if, for some co-workers,
"business as usual" means cheating or cutting corners.
People will always talk, and sometimes they'll gossip and
lie about us, our accomplishments, and our motives. The
following passage is adapted from a letter Ignatius wrote
to Isabel Roser. She and her husband gave alms generously,
but their neighbors repaid them with envy and calumny.

You speak of the enmities, intrigues, and untruths that have been circulated about you. I am not at all surprised at this, not even if it were worse than it is. For just as soon as you determined to bend every effort to secure the praise, honor, and service of God our Lord, you declared war against the world. You raised your standard in its face, and you got ready to reject what is lofty by embracing what is lowly, to accept indifferently honor and dishonor, riches and poverty, affection and hatred, welcome and repulse — in a word, the glory of the world or all the wrongs it could inflict upon you. We cannot be much afraid of the reproaches of this life when they are confined to words, for all the words in the world will never hurt a hair of our heads.

If we wish absolutely to live in honor and to be held in esteem by our neighbors, we can never be solidly rooted in God our Lord, and it will be impossible for us to remain unscathed when we meet their affronts.

My prayer for you is that you accept these affronts with patience and constancy. Remember the insults that Christ our Lord suffered for us.

I would rather fix my attention on one fault that I had committed than on all the evil that might be said of me. *Letters 11*

THINK ABOUT IT

- All the words in the world will never hurt a hair of our heads.
- How did Jesus respond when He was insulted and falsely accused?
- I would rather fix my attention on one fault I had committed than on all the evil that might be said of me.

JUST IMAGINE

"Blessed are those who are persecuted for righteousness' sake, for theirs is the kingdom of heaven. Blessed are you when people revile you and persecute you and utter all kinds of evil against you falsely on my account. Rejoice and be glad, for your reward is great in heaven, for in the same way they persecuted the prophets who were before you." MATTHEW 5:10-12

REMEMBER

If our primary concern is the esteem of our co-workers, we'll never be solidly rooted in God.

In advising people, St. Ignatius sometimes repeated the counsel: "Be slow to speak." In silence, he said, grow kindness, consideration, and understanding. Ill-considered words are often the source of our problems and even the occasion of many sins. In the Spiritual Exercises, *St. Ignatius highlighted the differences between idle and useful words.*

Among other sins of the tongue that we must avoid are idle words. No idle word should be uttered. I understand a word to be idle when it serves no good purpose, either for myself or for another, and was not intended to do so. Hence, words are never idle when spoken for any useful purpose, or when meant to serve the good of one's own soul or that of another, of the body or of temporal possessions. . . . In all we have mentioned, there will be merit if what is said is directed to some good purpose; there will be sin if it is directed to an evil purpose, or if engaged in for no good end.

Exercises, n. 40

THINK ABOUT IT

- I should strive to think before speaking.
- I should always use the gift of speech as a means of serving God and others.
- I should avoid speaking when my words would serve no good purpose for myself or for others.

If we put bits into the mouths of horses to make them obey us, we guide their whole bodies. Or look at ships: though they are so large that it takes strong winds to drive them, yet they are guided by a very small rudder wherever the will of the pilot directs. So also the tongue is a small member, yet it boasts of great exploits. How great a forest is set ablaze by a small fire! And the tongue is a fire. JAMES 3:3-6

REMEMBER

Among the sins of the tongue that we must avoid are idle words.

27. When Co-workers Are Downhearted

Perhaps we underestimate the effect we have on others. Just as lighting incense changes the air all around us, so lighting our smile can change the demeanor of the people nearby. Ignatius gave the following advice under the heading "How to negotiate and deal with others in our Lord."

We should charm those who are sad or tempted, speak at length and show great satisfaction and cheerfulness, both interior and exterior, so as to draw them to the opposite of what they feel, for their greater guidance and consolation.

Letters 52

THINK ABOUT IT

- I should be charming to those who are sad or tempted.
- Do my words and deeds show the inner satisfaction and cheer of someone who believes in Jesus Christ?
- Which co-workers would benefit from my smile today?

JUST IMAGINE

They cried out in fear. But immediately Jesus spoke to them and said, "Take heart, it is I; do not be afraid."

MATTHEW 14:26-27

When people are downhearted, our cheerfulness
should be their guidance and consolation.

28. Be a Peacemaker

We should not allow anger, dissatisfaction, or resentment to fester within us — or around us in the workplace. Ignatius wished no such divisions in the institutions he established.

Anger of some toward others should not be allowed among the residents of the house. If something of the sort arises, efforts should be made to bring the parties to prompt reconciliation and fitting satisfaction.

Constitutions, n. 275

THINK ABOUT IT

■ Do I belong to a faction in my workplace?

■ When co-workers speak angrily, I should not fuel their passion, but rather help them to understand the other point of view.

■ I must try to resolve my own feelings of bitterness, resentment, or anger.

JUST IMAGINE

Now I appeal to you, brothers and sisters, by the name of our Lord Jesus Christ, that all of you be in agreement and that there be no divisions among you, but that you be united in the same mind and the same purpose. For it has been reported to me . . . that there are quarrels among you, my brothers and sisters.

1 CORINTHIANS 1:10-11

REMEMBER

If anger arises, bring the parties to prompt reconciliation.

29. That All Might Be Saved

Everyone we know needs to draw closer to God; and, even if they are already nearer to Him than we are, God can use us to draw them still closer. Ignatius often pointed out that, in evangelization, our primary efforts should be toward those who are closest to us. The following appears in a letter to his brother Martin.

I have a great desire, a very great desire indeed, if I may say so, to see a true and intense love of God grow in you, my relatives and friends, so that you will bend all your efforts to the praise and service of God. Doing this, you make it possible for me to love you and serve you ever more and more, because in this service of the servants of my Lord there is for me both victory and glory.

Letters 7

THINK ABOUT IT

- I have a great desire to see a true and intense love of God grow in all my co-workers, relatives, and friends.
- I will imagine success in this way: when all of the people I know bend their efforts to the praise and service of God.
- Holiness makes people more worthy of love, more lovable.

God our Savior . . . desires everyone to be saved and to come to the knowledge of the truth.

1 TIMOTHY 2:3-4

In the service of the servants of my Lord, there is for me both victory and glory.

30. Good Deeds:
You *Can* Take Them With You

*Money doesn't make it to heaven. But prosperity — St.
Ignatius told his brother Martin — provides more opportunities for good deeds, which win for us "repose and
delight" in the afterlife.*

Share with some the influence of your family and
help others with money and goods. Deal with an
open hand with poor orphans and the needy. The
man with whom our Lord has been so generous
should not be miserly. One day we shall find in
heaven as much repose and delight as we have dispensed in this life; and since you can do so much
where you are, I beg of you again and again by the
love of our Lord Jesus Christ to make every effort
not only to give this matter some thought but to put
it into practice, because for those who love, nothing
is hard, especially when done for the love of our Lord
Jesus Christ.

Letters 8

THINK ABOUT IT

- I will share my influence, money, and goods. I
  will deal with an open hand.
- We shall find in heaven as much repose and
  delight as we have dispensed in this life.
- For those who love, nothing is hard, especially
  when done for the love of our Lord Jesus Christ.

And I heard a voice from heaven saying, "Write this: Blessed are the dead who from now on die in the Lord." "Yes," says the Spirit, "they will rest from their labors, for their deeds follow them."

REVELATION 14:13

REMEMBER

Those with whom our Lord has been so generous should not be miserly.

31. Work With What You Have

The more you have materially, the more money you earn, the greater your authority over others, the more you will be held accountable for your example and your charity. So said Ignatius to his prosperous brother.

I beg of you by God's reverence and love to make every effort to win honor in heaven, fame and renown before the Lord, Who is going to be our judge. For if He has given you an abundance of this world's goods, it is to help you earn those of heaven by giving a good example and sound teaching to your sons, servants, and relatives. Converse spiritually with some, impose a proper punishment on others, without anger or harshness.

Letters 8

THINK ABOUT IT

- Have I made the best use of the material goods God has given me?
- I have a duty to give good example, advice, and admonition to the people over whom I have authority, at work and in the family.
- Do I reprimand people — when necessary — in a way that is charitable and respectful of their dignity?

"Do not store up for yourselves treasures on earth, where moth and rust consume and where thieves break in and steal; but store up for yourselves treasures in heaven, where neither moth nor rust consumes and where thieves do not break in and steal. For where your treasure is, there your heart will be also."

MATTHEW 6:19-21

If God has given you an abundance of this world's goods, it is to help you earn those of heaven.

32. People Before Paychecks

Ignatius wrote the following to his great benefactor Isabel Roser.

Be sure that your solid and sincere affection for me will bring me as much spiritual joy as if you sent me all the money in the world. Our Lord insists that we look to the giver and love him more than his gift, and thus keep him ever before our eyes and in the most intimate thoughts of our heart.

Letters 10

THINK ABOUT IT

- I must be grateful to those who provide, directly and indirectly, for my well-being: my employer, my customers, my co-workers.
- I must strive to love others more perfectly, and not merely for what they give me.
- I should pray daily for my benefactors.

JUST IMAGINE

May the Lord grant mercy to the household of Onesiphorus, because he often refreshed me and was not ashamed of my chain; when he arrived in Rome, he eagerly searched for me and found me — may the Lord grant that he will find mercy from the Lord on that day! And you know very well how much service he rendered in Ephesus. 2 TIMOTHY 1:16-18

REMEMBER

Love the giver more than the gift.

33. Setting the Standard

It can be most difficult to get perspective on oneself. In the
Spiritual Exercises, *St. Ignatius offers us three imaginative ways to do so.*

I should place before my mind a person . . . whom I
wish to be wholly perfect in the office and state of
life which he occupies. Now the same standard of
action that I would like him to follow in his way of
distributing alms for the greater glory of God and
the perfection of his soul I myself will observe, and do
neither more nor less. I shall abide myself by the same
rule I would like him to follow, and the norm I judge
would be for the glory of God.

I should picture myself at the hour of my death,
and ponder well the way and norm I would then wish
to have kept in carrying out the duties of my office. I
will lay down the same rule for myself now, and keep
it in my distribution of alms.

I should imagine myself before my judge on the
last day, and weigh well the manner in which I would
wish then to have done my duty in carrying out this
office. The same rule that I would then wish to have
observed I will keep now.

Exercises, nn. 339-341

THINK ABOUT IT

■ Do I judge myself by the same standard I use to
judge others?

- I must live (and give) as if today were my last day and my judgment by God tomorrow.
- If I were to be judged today, what might God say about my generosity and my sense of duty?

JUST IMAGINE

"When the Son of Man comes in his glory, and all the angels with him, then he will sit on the throne of his glory. All the nations will be gathered before him, and he will separate people one from another as a shepherd separates the sheep from the goats, and he will put the sheep at his right hand and the goats at the left. Then the king will say to those at his right hand, 'Come, you that are blessed by my Father, inherit the kingdom prepared for you from the foundation of the world; for I was hungry and you gave me food, I was thirsty and you gave me something to drink, I was a stranger and you welcomed me, I was naked and you gave me clothing, I was sick and you took care of me, I was in prison and you visited me.' Then the righteous will answer him, 'Lord, when was it that we saw you hungry . . . or thirsty . . .? And when was it that we saw you a stranger and welcomed you, or naked and gave you clothing? And when was it that we saw you sick or in prison and visited you?' And the king will answer them, 'Truly I tell you, just as you did it to one of the least of these who are members of my family, you did it to me.' " MATTHEW 25:31-40

I should picture myself at the hour of my death, and ponder the way I would have wished I had carried out my duties. I will lay down the same rule for myself now.

34. To Speak Up or Keep Silent?

We must depend upon the Holy Spirit to lead us to speak or keep silent. God knows the hearts of the people around us and wants them to be saved, not scandalized. He will guide us.

We may often have to control the desire we feel and speak less of the things of God our Lord; at other times we may speak more than the satisfaction or movement we feel prompts us to. We act thus because in this matter we should give more heed to the good of others than to our own desires. When the enemy thus tries to magnify or diminish the communication received, we must proceed for the purpose of helping others, like a man who is crossing a ford. If I find a good footing — that is, some way or hope of profiting the neighbor — I will pass right on. But if the ford is muddied or disturbed and there is danger that scandal may be taken from what I say, I will rein in and seek an occasion more favorable to what I have to say.

Letters 23

THINK ABOUT IT

■ We may often have to control the desire we feel and speak less of the things of God.

■ At other times, we must speak up, even though we would prefer to shut up.

■ I must determine, in prayer, the best way to serve the person who is with me.

They went through the region of Phrygia and Galatia, having been forbidden by the Holy Spirit to speak the word in Asia. When they had come opposite Mysia, they attempted to go into Bithynia, but the Spirit of Jesus did not allow them; so, passing by Mysia, they went down to Troas.   ACTS 16:6-8

If there is danger that scandal may be taken from what I say, I will rein in and seek a more favorable occasion.

35. Obeying the Teaching Church

Obedience to the teaching Church — and especially the Pope — is a distinguishing mark of Ignatius's spirituality. Ignatius said that if he saw something as white, and the Church defined it as black, he would believe it black. We should earnestly study and obey the Church's teachings that apply to our particular profession. The following is the first of Ignatius's "Rules for Thinking with the Church."

We must put aside all judgment of our own and keep the mind ever ready and prompt to obey in all things the true Spouse of Christ our Lord, our holy Mother, the hierarchical Church.

Exercises, n. 353

THINK ABOUT IT

- I must study the teachings of the Church that apply to my daily work.
- Have I been disobedient to the Church, or redefined "obedience" so as to make it absurd?
- How do I show my love for the Pope, the successor of Peter, the prince of the apostles?

JUST IMAGINE

And Jesus answered him, "Blessed are you, Simon son of Jonah! For flesh and blood has not revealed this to you, but my Father in heaven. And I tell you, you are Peter, and on this rock I will build my church, and the gates of Hades will not prevail against it. I will give you the keys of the kingdom of heaven, and whatever you bind on earth will be bound in heaven, and whatever you loose on earth will be loosed in heaven."   MATTHEW 16:17-19

REMEMBER

We must put aside all judgment of our own and keep the mind ever prompt to obey the hierarchical Church.

We're all asked to do work we'd rather not do — work that's not in our job description. Ignatius saw this as a blessing, helping us to grow in virtue.

It will be very specially helpful to perform with all possible devotion the tasks in which humility and charity are practiced more.... The more one binds oneself to God our Lord and shows himself more generous toward His Divine Majesty, the more will he find God more generous toward himself and the more disposed will he be to receive graces and spiritual gifts which are greater each day.

Constitutions, n. 282

THINK ABOUT IT

- Do I reject necessary tasks because I think they are beneath my dignity?
- When I am generous in performing these tasks, I am generous toward my neighbor and toward God.
- Menial work, done willingly, makes me better disposed to receive God's graces.

JUST IMAGINE

Paul left Athens and went to Corinth. There he found a Jew named Aquila, a native of Pontus, who had recently come from Italy with his wife Priscilla, because Claudius had ordered all Jews to leave Rome.

Paul went to see them, and, because he was of the same trade, he stayed with them, and they worked together — by trade they were tentmakers.

ACTS 18:1-3

REMEMBER

It will be very specially helpful to perform with all possible devotion the tasks in which humility and charity are practiced more.

37. Keep Busy and Out of Trouble

Ignatius set this for all time as a rule for his community.

Idleness, which is the source of all evils, should have no place in any of our houses.

Constitutions, n. 253

- When I am surprised by free time, do I fill it up with good activity?
- I will examine the amount of time I waste in passive and useless entertainment, such as television. Do I waste too much of my life this way?
- I will root out idleness as I would root out the evils it produces.

JUST IMAGINE

Now we command you, beloved, in the name of our Lord Jesus Christ, to keep away from believers who are living in idleness and not according to the tradition that they received from us. For you yourselves know how you ought to imitate us; we were not idle when we were with you, and we did not eat anyone's bread without paying for it; but with toil and labor we worked night and day, so that we might not burden any of you. This was not because we do not have that right, but in order to give you an example to imitate. For even when we were with you, we gave you this command: Anyone unwilling to work should not eat. For we hear that some of you are living in idleness, mere busybodies, not doing any work. Now such persons we command and exhort in the Lord Jesus Christ to do their work quietly and to earn their own living.

2 THESSALONIANS 3:6-12

REMEMBER

Idleness is the source of all evils.

38. Asking for a Raise

Ignatius gave the following advice to Archbishop John Peter Caraffa, who later became Pope Paul IV. Founders and archbishops, like lay people in families, need to provide for their households, their Church, and God's poor. There comes a time when we must pray for the courage to ask for a raise.

St. Francis and others of the blessed who thought they had as much confidence and trust in God did not for this reason neglect to take proper means to see that their houses were preserved and grew in number for the greater service and praise of the Divine Majesty. To do otherwise would have seemed to them rather to tempt the Lord they aimed at serving and to act in a way that would not be in keeping with His service.

Letters 28

THINK ABOUT IT

- Am I receiving a just wage for the work I do?
- Do I have a realistic chance of getting the money I deserve — or need — for the sake of my family?
- Do I refrain from asking about money because I am ashamed, cowardly, or sinfully proud?

JUST IMAGINE

Do we not have the right to our food and drink? . . . Who plants a vineyard and does not eat any of its fruit? Or who tends a flock and does not get any of its milk? Do I say this on human authority? Does not the law also say the same? For it is written in the law of Moses, "You shall not muzzle an ox while it is treading out the grain." Is it for oxen that God is concerned? Or does he not speak entirely for our sake? It was indeed written for our sake, for whoever plows should plow in hope and whoever threshes should thresh in hope of a share in the crop.

1 CORINTHIANS 9:4, 7-10

REMEMBER

St. Francis and others who trusted God did not neglect to take proper means to see that their houses were preserved for the greater service and praise of God.

39. Against Presumption

Though planning is good, it is possible to overdo it — to delude ourselves into thinking we're in control of everything. We should make plans, yes, but we should trust that God has a plan of His own. The following anecdote appears in Father Luis González de Cámara's preface to Ignatius's autobiography.

When he heard anyone saying, "I will do this two weeks from now, or a week from now," the Father [Ignatius] was always a bit amazed: "How's that? Do you count on living that long?"

THINK ABOUT IT

- I must remember that all I have is a gift from God — my life, my possessions, my successes — and not presume that any of these are mine by right.
- How do I react when unexpected events upset my plans?
- Do I trust that God has a plan for me and my work?

JUST IMAGINE

Come now, you who say, "Today or tomorrow we will go to such and such a town and spend a year there, doing business and making money." Yet you do not even know what tomorrow will bring. What is your life? For you are a mist that appears for a little while and then vanishes. Instead you ought to say, "If the Lord wishes, we will live and do this or that."

JAMES 4:13-15

"You know neither the day nor the hour" (Matthew 25:13).

40. Nothing's Going Right!

The early Jesuits experienced many successes, but more than their share of failures and frustrations as well. Ignatius consoled Father Louis de Calatayud, who was trying to establish a college and getting nowhere.

I saw what annoyance and discouragement... this work is costing you. I should think that God's divine and supreme goodness wishes to give you the fullest and most abundant reward in His kingdom for the service you are doing Him. For where others are accustomed to find consolation and support in their good works even from other people, you have found annoyance and such extraordinary opposition. The love of God our Lord and of your neighbor which moves you must be especially pure and courageous, for only such a love could make you persevere where forces so opposed are found to embarrass you. And yet I hope in God our Lord that with the example of others this attempt will have a better ending than is augured by its beginnings....

Letters 433

THINK ABOUT IT

- If I work faithfully now, my primary reward will be in God's kingdom.
- When others oppose me, I have an opportunity to be more like Jesus Christ.

■ God does not ask us to succeed, but to be faithful.

While Paul was waiting for them in Athens, he was deeply distressed to see that the city was full of idols. So he argued in the synagogue with the Jews and the devout persons, and also in the marketplace every day with those who happened to be there. Also some Epicurean and Stoic philosophers debated with him. . . . When they heard of the resurrection of the dead, some scoffed. . . . At that point Paul left them.

ACTS 17:16-18, 32-33

REMEMBER

The love of God that moves you must be especially pure and courageous, for only such a love could make you persevere.

41. How God Teaches

When Ignatius suffered adversity, he always assumed that God was trying to teach him something. Some lessons are difficult, and they can only be learned the hard way.

At this time God treated [Ignatius] just as a schoolmaster treats a little boy when he teaches him. This perhaps was because of his rough and uncultivated understanding, or because he had no one to teach him, or because of the firm will God Himself had given him in His service. But he clearly saw, and always had seen that God dealt with him like this. Rather, he thought that any doubt about it would be an offense against His Divine Majesty.

Autobiography, n. 27

THINK ABOUT IT

- I should look for the lessons in my troubles.
- Do I blame the methods of my divine Teacher when it is I who am reluctant and slow to learn my lessons?
- God teaches me in the way best suited to me.

JUST IMAGINE

"Learn from me; for I am gentle and humble in heart, and you will find rest for your souls. For my yoke is easy, and my burden is light."   MATTHEW 11:29-30

God treats me just as a schoolteacher treats a little student.

Ignatius helped many of his contemporaries advance to the summit of holiness. He gave the following counsel in a 1546 letter to Peter Canisius, then a young Jesuit. The Church declared Peter a saint in 1925.

Courage, then, courage! Be comforted in the Lord and in the strength of His power (Ephesians 6:10), which is Christ Jesus our Lord and God. He died for our sins (1 Corinthians 15:3) and rose for our justification (Romans 4:25). And He has given us life together with Him, and He has caused us to sit with Him in heaven (Ephesians 2:6), in God. Study and ponder the vocation to which you have been called. Make use of the grace which in Christ has been given you (Romans 12:3), keep close to it, trade with it, never allow it to remain idle in you, never resist it. The same Lord it is who works in us both to will and to accomplish, according to His good will (Philippians 2:13), which is in itself infinite and all-glorious and ineffable for us through Christ Jesus. For the Spirit of Jesus will give you understanding (2 Timothy 2:7) and fortitude in all things, so that through you the name of Jesus will be glorified and bear much fruit in many souls, with the hope of a better life.

Letters 97

- I live in the Lord and in the strength of His power.
- God has called me to a particular way of life. I must study and ponder this vocation.
- God Who called me will give me the courage and strength to answer His call.

JUST IMAGINE

While [Jesus] was still speaking, some people came from the leader's house to say, "Your daughter is dead. Why trouble the teacher any further?" But overhearing what they said, Jesus said to the leader of the synagogue, "Do not fear, only believe." MARK 5:35-36

REMEMBER

Be comforted in the Lord and in the strength of His power.

God is served by hard work and by dedicated work, but not by workaholism. Ignatius wrote of moderation to a group of young people who were going too far in the demands they placed on their bodies.

"Nothing in excess," said the philosopher. . . . If one fails to observe this moderation, he will find that good is turned into evil and virtue into vice. He will also learn that many inconveniences follow which are quite contrary to the purpose of the one who so acts.

The first is that God is not really served in the long run, as the horse worn out in the first days does not, as a rule, finish the journey, and thus it happens that someone must be found to care for it.

Second, gains that are made with this excessive eagerness are not usually kept, as Scripture says, "Wealth hastily gotten will dwindle" (Proverbs 13:11). Not only dwindle, but it may be the cause of a fall: "And one who moves too hurriedly misses the way" (Proverbs 19:2); and if he missteps, the further he falls, the greater the danger, for he will not stop until he has reached the bottom of the ladder.

Third, there is the danger of being careless about overloading the vessel. There is danger, of course, in sailing it empty, as it can then be tossed about on the waves of temptation. But there is also danger of so overloading it as to cause it to sink.

Letters 126-127

- If I fail to observe moderation, I will turn good into evil and virtue into vice.
- One who moves too hurriedly misses the way.
- I must take care not to sail with a vessel that is empty, or one that is overloaded.

JUST IMAGINE

"Come to me, all you that are weary and are carrying heavy burdens, and I will give you rest."

MATTHEW 11:28

REMEMBER

The horse worn out in the first days does not, as a rule, finish the journey.

Sickness should provide us opportunities for growth and good example — not self-pity and self-indulgence. The following counsel is adapted from Ignatius's Constitutions of the Society of Jesus, *n. 272.*

Try to draw fruit from your illnesses, not only for yourself but for the edification of others. Do not be impatient or difficult to please. Rather, have and show much patience and obedience to your doctor and whoever is taking care of you. And use good and edifying words that show that the sickness is accepted as a gift from the hand of our Creator and Lord, since sickness is a gift not less than health.

THINK ABOUT IT

- When I am sick, I should share the Gospel and not my misery.
- I should follow the instructions of my doctor or others who know better.
- Do I look upon sickness as a gift?

JUST IMAGINE

We are children of God, and if children, then heirs, heirs of God and joint heirs with Christ — if, in fact, we suffer with him so that we may also be glorified with him. I consider that the sufferings of this present time are not worth comparing with the glory about to be revealed to us. ROMANS 8:16-18

Sickness is a gift not less than health.

45. Take Care of Yourself

Father Anthony Araoz was a nephew of St. Ignatius and a close friend. He was the first Spanish Jesuit to work in Spain, where he served as provincial. He was a hard worker — in fact, he was somewhat workaholic. Ignatius heard that his nephew was not eating properly, couldn't sleep, and was feeling weak. So the founder tried first to nudge him toward more healthy habits. When this failed, Ignatius commanded him to take care of his health.

I have been informed of the great need you have to look after your health, something I have partially known. I do know that though your health is frail, you allow yourself to be carried away by your charity to undertake tasks and labors that are more than you can conveniently bear. Judging in God our Lord that it would be more acceptable to His Divine Majesty to have you temper your zeal in this respect so that you will be able to labor the longer in His service, I have deemed it proper in our Lord to command you to follow the physician's advice in all that pertains to your meals, the use of your time, what hours and when you are to take for sleep and repose. For the next three months, from now until September, you are to do no preaching, but are to look after your health. An occasional exception may be made, if . . . you can do so once a month without injury to your health.

Letters 243-244

- I must learn to trust others and ask them to share my work when I cannot do it myself.
- I must learn to trust God and not believe that the fate of the world rests with me alone.
- I must not work myself sick.
- Who am I trying to impress?

No longer drink only water, but take a little wine for the sake of your stomach and your frequent ailments.

1 TIMOTHY 5:23

Temper your zeal so that you will be able to labor longer in God's service.

46. The Grass Seems Greener Over There

The food on the other plate usually looks tastier. The faults of others seem more easily fixed than our own. This is fallen human nature, against which we must be on guard. Thus Ignatius counseled his community at Alcalá, Spain.

The enemy is wont to tempt those in the desert with thoughts of dealing with the neighbor and improving him, and to those who are helping the neighbor he will propose the great perfection of the desert and solitary life. Thus he lays hold of what is far off to prevent us from taking advantage of what is at hand.

Letters 440

THINK ABOUT IT

- Am I more aware of the faults of others than I am of my own faults?
- Do I waste time wishing I had the vocation or opportunities that others have, instead of attending to the duties I have before me?
- I must try to live in the present moment, where God's will for me is real.

JUST IMAGINE

"Why do you see the speck in your neighbor's eye, but do not notice the log in your own eye? Or how can you say to your neighbor, 'Let me take the speck out of your eye,' while the log is in your own eye? You hypocrite, first take the log out of your own eye, and then you will see clearly to take the speck out of your neighbor's eye."   MATTHEW 7:3-5

REMEMBER

The enemy lays hold of what is far off to prevent us from taking advantage of what is at hand.

47. Self-Pity and Discouragement

Ignatius's counsel to Sister Teresa Rejadella shows a keen understanding of human psychology and demonic subtlety. The devil knows our weaknesses better than we know them ourselves. We should abhor self-pity. And we should not depend upon consolations and comforts when we are suffering.

Our ancient enemy sets up all possible obstacles to turn us aside from the way on which we have entered. He makes use of everything to vex us, and everything in the first lesson is reversed. We find ourselves sad without knowing why. We cannot pray with devotion, nor contemplate, nor even speak or hear of the things of God with any interior taste or relish. Not only this, but if he sees that we are weak and much humbled by these harmful thoughts, he goes on to suggest that we are entirely forgotten by God our Lord, and leads us to think that we are quite separated from Him and that all that we have done and all that we desire to do is entirely worthless. He thus endeavors to bring us to a state of general discouragement. We can thus see what causes our fear and weakness: it is a too-prolonged gaze at such times on our miseries. We allow ourselves to be laid low by his misleading suggestions. For this reason it is necessary for us to be aware of our opponent. If we are in consolation, we should abase and humble ourselves and reflect that soon the trial of temptation will come. And when temptation, darkness, or sadness comes upon us, we must go contrary to it without permitting ourselves to pay any attention to the unpleasant impressions caused in us, and hope patiently for the consolation of our Lord, which will cast out all our uneasiness and scatter all the clouds.

Letters 22

THINK ABOUT IT

- Do I rely too much on good feelings and consolations in my prayer?
- I must not dwell too long on my miseries, but rather on the sufferings of Jesus.
- I must fight temptation as soon as I discern it.

JUST IMAGINE

Discipline yourselves, keep alert. Like a roaring lion your adversary the devil prowls around, looking for someone to devour.   1 PETER 5:8

REMEMBER

We can see what causes our fear and weakness: it is a too-prolonged gaze on our miseries.

48. Anxiety About Spiritual Things

Ignatius counsels a brother Jesuit, Jerome Vines, not to worry overmuch about his limitations and shortcomings in prayer, but to trust more in God.

Concerning method of prayer . . . do what you can calmly and gently. Do not be disturbed about the rest, but leave to God's providence what you cannot manage yourself. God is well pleased with the earnestness and moderate anxiety with which we attend to our obligations, but He is not pleased with that anxiety which afflicts the soul, because He wishes our limitations and weakness to seek the support of His strength and omnipotence, with the trust that in His goodness He will supply what is lacking to our weakness and shortcomings.

If one is involved in much business, even though his intention be good and holy, he must make up his mind to do what he can, without afflicting himself if he cannot do all that he wishes. Let him do all that a man ought to do who follows the dictate of a good conscience. If other things permit, you must have patience and not think that God our Lord requires what man cannot accomplish, nor that He wishes you to be cast down. And if one satisfies God, what difference does it make whether he satisfies men? There is no need to wear yourself out, but make a competent and sufficient effort, and leave the rest to Him Who can do all He pleases. *Letters 404-405*

- God is pleased with the earnestness we give to our duties, but He is not pleased with anxiety that afflicts the soul.
- In my weakness, I will seek God's strength.
- God never requires what I cannot accomplish, nor does He wish me to be downcast.

JUST IMAGINE

Jesus spoke to them and said, "Take heart, it is I; do not be afraid." Peter answered him, "Lord, if it is you, command me to come to you on the water." He said, "Come." So Peter got out of the boat, started walking on the water, and came toward Jesus. But when he noticed the strong wind, he became frightened, and beginning to sink, he cried out, "Lord, save me!" Jesus immediately reached out his hand and caught him.

MATTHEW 14:27-31

REMEMBER

There is no need to wear yourself out, but make a competent and sufficient effort, and leave the rest to Him Who can do all He pleases.

49. When We Are Ashamed

God allows us to make humiliating mistakes, because that is how we learn humility. Our mistakes help us to know ourselves better, know our limitations, and know our foibles and our bluster. Ignatius told the community at Alcalá, Spain, how best to deal with embarrassment and shame.

Should anyone do anything that is disedifying, and it seems that as a result he should be held in less esteem than he was held before, let him not be so discouraged as to wish to give up, but let him humble himself and ask forgiveness of those who might have been scandalized by his bad example.... He should give thanks to God Who has permitted him to be humbled, so that he can be known by all for what he is. He should not wish to appear better in the eyes of men than he is in the eyes of God. The brethren who behold him should think that they could fall into even greater weakness, and should ask God to strengthen them.   *Letters 440*

THINK ABOUT IT

- I must seek forgiveness when I make mistakes, even if it means drawing attention to my errors.
- I should give thanks to God for humiliations, even if I don't *feel* thankful.
- I should seek to forgive others promptly and learn from their mistakes as if I myself had been humbled.

"Father, I have sinned against heaven and before you; I am no longer worthy to be called your son; treat me like one of your hired hands."   LUKE 15:18-19

I should not wish to appear better in the eyes of others than I am in the eyes of God.

50. Don't Blame Others

It's always easy to find excuses for why we're failing in our work. We can blame the system, our co-workers, the boss, the absentee owner, our genetic makeup, our upbringing. A young student named Bartholomew Romano wrote to Ignatius listing all the reasons he was not advancing as he should. He blamed his workload, his superiors, and his confreres. Ignatius's response is bracing. He tells Bartholomew that he must change his conduct and not his place of residence. Bartholomew's problem was coming from inside, and unless that part of him changed, he would never be happy anywhere.

You are mistaken in thinking that the cause of your disquiet, or little progress in the Lord, is due to the place, or your superiors, or your brethren. This disquiet comes from within and not from without. I mean from your lack of humility, obedience, prayer, and your slight mortification — in a word, your little fervor in advancing in the way of perfection. You could change residence, superiors, and brethren, but if you do not change the interior man, you will never do good. And you will everywhere be the same, unless you succeed in being humble, obedient, devout, and mortified in your self-love. This is the only change you should seek. I mean that you should try to change the interior man and lead him back like a servant to God.

Letters 363

■ When I am troubled, where do I begin looking for the causes?
■ What are the obstacles to my spiritual progress?
■ What are the changes I'd like to make? What are the changes I need to make?

JUST IMAGINE

Then [Jesus] called the crowd again and said to them, "Listen to me, all of you, and understand: there is nothing outside a person that by going in can defile, but the things that come out are what defile. . . . It is what comes out of a person that defiles. For it is from within, from the human heart, that evil intentions come: fornication, theft, murder, adultery, avarice, wickedness, deceit, licentiousness, envy, slander, pride, folly. All these evil things come from within, and they defile a person."   MARK 7:14-15, 20-23

REMEMBER

This is the only change you should seek: You should try to change the interior man and lead him back like a servant to God.

51. The Temptation of the Future

Advice for living today comes from Ignatius's "Rules for dealing with others," written for the Jesuit community at Alcalá, Spain.

We should never postpone a good work, no matter how small it may be, with the thought of later doing something greater. It is a very common temptation of the enemy to be always placing before us the perfection of things to come and bring us to make little of the present.   *Letters 440*

THINK ABOUT IT

- I must avoid the temptation to romanticize the future and waste my time in daydreams.
- I cannot recover the time I waste today. It is lost forever.
- God has given me today to spend in His service. He may not give me tomorrow.

JUST IMAGINE

"So do not worry about tomorrow, for tomorrow will bring worries of its own. Today's trouble is enough for today."   MATTHEW 6:34

REMEMBER

It is a common temptation of the enemy to place before us the perfection of things to come and bring us to make little of the present.

52. Encourage Your Critics

Ignatius considered it an act of charity to correct someone who was sinning or mistaken. He urged others to be just as direct in correcting his faults. He wrote the following to his brother Martin.

It is with this solid love and honest desire that I speak, write, and advise you just as I should honestly wish and desire you to advise, urge, and correct me.

Letters 7

THINK ABOUT IT

- I should accept criticism gratefully, even when it is not delivered well.
- I should try not to make excuses or arguments when friends or co-workers correct me.
- I should pray to God about how I might improve from my co-workers' corrections.

JUST IMAGINE

The Lord's servant must not be quarrelsome but kindly to everyone, an apt teacher, patient, correcting opponents with gentleness.   2 TIMOTHY 2:24-25

REMEMBER

I should speak, write, and advise others just as I should honestly wish others to advise, urge, and correct me.

Ignatius was a true friend, whose correction and encouragement hastened others on their way to holiness. We should be the same kind of friend. And we should seek out the same sort of friend, who will be frank with us.

To make progress in the practice of virtue, it is of great advantage to have a friend, whom you yourself have chosen, to advise you of your faults.

Woodstock

THINK ABOUT IT

- I must cultivate honesty in my friends.
- I should seek out a friend who shares my beliefs, to advise me on ways to improve myself.
- I should try, as well as I can, to track my growth in particular virtues so that I do not stand still or fall backward.

JUST IMAGINE

Therefore confess your sins to one another, and pray for one another, so that you may be healed. . . . You should know that whoever brings back a sinner from wandering will save the sinner's soul from death and will cover a multitude of sins.   JAMES 5:16, 20

REMEMBER

Have a friend who will advise you of your faults.

*Ignatius spoke plainly and avoided the melodramatic —
and potentially blasphemous — act of swearing. He swore
oaths only in cases where he was required, as in a court of
law. His advice in this matter is included in the* Catechism of the Catholic Church, *n. 2164.*

Do not swear, whether by the Creator or any crea-
ture, except truthfully, of necessity, and with reverence.

By reverence I mean that when the name of the
Creator and Lord is mentioned, one acts with consideration and devoutly manifests due honor and
respect.

Exercises, n. 38

- I must not swear oaths casually or unnecessarily.
- I must use God's name and titles only with reverence, and never as curses or with profanity.
- I should use God's name and titles as short, silent
  prayers during the workday.

"But I say to you, Do not swear at all, either by
heaven, for it is the throne of God, or by the earth, for
it is his footstool, or by Jerusalem, for it is the city of
the great King. And do not swear by your head, for
you cannot make one hair white or black. Let your

word be 'Yes, Yes' or 'No, No'; anything more than this comes from the evil one."   MATTHEW 5:34-37

When the name of the Creator and Lord is mentioned, one should act with consideration and devoutly show due honor and respect.

55. Make Time for Quiet

Those who wish to advance in the spiritual life must try to make time for a retreat. For good reason, Ignatius is the patron saint of spiritual retreats. He saw these times in silence as opportunities for conversion. Can you spare a long weekend or a few vacation days for the Lord?

If in order to serve and praise God our Lord, one withdraws from numerous friends and acquaintances and from many occupations not undertaken with a pure intention, he gains no little merit before the Divine Majesty.

In this seclusion, the mind is not engaged in many things, but can give its whole attention to one single interest — that is, to the service of its Creator and its spiritual progress. Thus it is more free to use its natural powers to seek diligently what it so much desires.

The more the soul is in solitude and seclusion, the more fit it renders itself to approach and be united with its Creator and Lord; and the more closely it is united with Him, the more it disposes itself to receive graces and gifts from the infinite goodness of its God.

Exercises, n. 20

THINK ABOUT IT

- I should schedule regular times of quiet prayer, daily if possible.
- I should try to make an annual retreat.

■ In quiet time, I should try to give my whole attention to serving God.

Now during those days [Jesus] went out to the mountain to pray; and he spent the night in prayer to God.

LUKE 6:12

The more the soul is in solitude and seclusion, the more fit it renders itself to approach and be united with its Creator and Lord.

56. Never Alone

St. Ignatius drew up a set of rules for those who were beginning an ambitious task — the founding of a college. Amidst the busyness, he said, they should take care to remind themselves that they are always in God's presence.

We should not wish to see or do anything which could not be done in the presence of God and His creatures, and we shall thus imagine that we are always in His presence.   *Letters 440*

THINK ABOUT IT

■ I am always in the presence of God.
■ When I sin, I behave foolishly, as if God could not see me.
■ Because I cannot see God, I must find ways to remind myself of His presence — a sacred image, perhaps, or some words on a piece of paper in my line of sight.

JUST IMAGINE

"Your Father who sees in secret . . . knows what you need before you ask him."   MATTHEW 6:6, 8

REMEMBER

We wish not to see or do anything that could not be done in the presence of God.

Ignatius offered strong words against Father Andrew Oviedo, one of the early Jesuits. Father Oviedo wished himself to be a hermit and taught that the active soul should strive to experience God's presence in a way that is intense and constant. Ignatius argued that such prayer, which is proper to the life of a hermit, might be incompatible with a life in the world.

What he [Oviedo] says of the supernatural manner of prayer, in which the presence of God is continual, seems fantastic and erroneous. Such a thing is not seen in the lives of even the greatest saints, although they have a recollection of God which is more frequent, a consideration of God more real than most men. Such continuity, however, is impossible in the ordinary course of things, even with the most spiritual and saintly man. Such a presence would demand a fixed, immobile attention of the mind which is repugnant to our state as *viatores* [wayfarers in the world, pilgrims on the way to heaven].

Modern 152

THINK ABOUT IT

- I should thank God, at all times, for the particular vocation He has reserved for me.
- I should not compare my vocation with those of others and wish for things that are not properly mine.

■ I should study, pray, and seek spiritual direction in order to grow in the particular way that God intends for me.

JUST IMAGINE

There is one body and one Spirit, just as you were called to the one hope of your calling. . . . But each of us was given grace according to the measure of Christ's gift. . . . The gifts he gave were that some would be apostles, some prophets, some evangelists, some pastors and teachers, to equip the saints for the work of ministry, for building up the body of Christ, until all of us come to the unity of the faith and of the knowledge of the Son of God, to maturity, to the measure of the full stature of Christ.

EPHESIANS 4:4, 7, 11-13

REMEMBER

The way of prayer that is proper to hermits is impossible in the ordinary course of things, even for the most spiritual and most saintly.

58. Seeing Clearly

We must never excuse our sins because they "cause no harm" to others. They are sins against almighty God, Who loves us, Who became human, and Who died for us.

I will consider Who God is against Whom I have sinned, going through His attributes and comparing them with their contraries in me: His wisdom with my ignorance, His power with my weakness, His justice with my iniquity, His goodness with my wickedness.   *Exercises*, n. 59

THINK ABOUT IT

■ God knows everything. What do I know? How often do I find myself mistaken?

■ God is all-powerful. What can I do? How often do I fail or fall short?

■ God is good and just. How often do I sin in thoughts, words, and deeds?

JUST IMAGINE

Simon Peter . . . fell down at Jesus' knees, saying, "Go away from me, Lord, for I am a sinful man!" . . . Then Jesus said to Simon, "Do not be afraid."

LUKE 5:8, 10

REMEMBER

I will consider Who God is, and who I am.

59. Driving Out Vice

Father Pedro de Ribadeneira, Ignatius's secretary, preserved the following saying of his master.

In order to replace a bad habit with a good one, you must use effort upon effort, just as you use one nail to drive out another.

Woodstock

THINK ABOUT IT

■ What is my dominant fault — the sin or defect that most leads me to commit other sins?
■ What is the virtue that opposes my dominant fault?
■ What is the best way for me to grow in that virtue, so that, with God's help, I drive out my bad habits?

JUST IMAGINE

For those whom he foreknew he also predestined to be conformed to the image of his Son.

ROMANS 8:29

REMEMBER

In order to replace a bad habit with a good one, you must use effort upon effort, just as you use one nail to drive out another.

60. Back to the Basics

Ignatius exhorted the citizens of his hometown to "restore and renew" the traditions of Catholic piety.

Let it be our glory, then, out of love for so good a Lord and because of the immense benefit to our souls, to restore and renew in some way the holy practices of our ancestors; if not entirely, at least in part, to the extent of monthly confession and Communion, as I have already suggested. Should one wish to go oftener than this, there is no doubt that he would be acting in conformity with the wish of our Creator and Lord.

Letters 45

THINK ABOUT IT

■ I must make an effort to understand the traditions of Christian prayer.
■ I should not reject traditional practices that I have not taken the time to understand.
■ I should go to confession at least once a month, if not more often.

JUST IMAGINE

You need someone to teach you again the basic elements of the oracles of God. You need milk, not solid food.   HEBREWS 5:12

Let it be our glory to restore and renew the holy practices of our ancestors.

61. Praying the Lord's Prayer

Ignatius counsels us to meditate occasionally on the words and phrases of the prayer that Jesus taught His disciples.

METHOD: ... One may kneel or sit, as may be better suited to his disposition and more conducive to devotion. He should keep his eyes closed, or fixed in one position without permitting them to roam. Then let him say, "Father," and continue meditating upon this word as long as he finds various meanings, comparisons, relish, and consolation in the consideration of it. The same method should be followed with each word of the Our Father, or of any other prayer which he wishes to use for this method.

If in contemplation, he finds in one or two words abundant matter for thought and much relish and consolation, he should not be anxious to go on, though the whole hour be taken up with what he has found. When the hour is over, let him say the rest of the Our Father in the usual way.

If he has been occupied with one or two words of the Our Father for a whole hour, when he wishes to pray on another day, let him say those words in the ordinary way, and begin to contemplate with the words that follow immediately after them.

Exercises, nn. 252-255

- I must come to know the Our Father as the perfect prayer, because it has come from God Himself.
- In the course of my lifetime, I must come to know and love each word of the Lord's Prayer.
- I should give some thought to the posture and dispositions that are most conducive to my prayer.

JUST IMAGINE

[One of Jesus'] disciples said to him, "Lord, teach us to pray, as John taught his disciples." He said to them, "When you pray, say:
    Father, hallowed be your name.
        Your kingdom come.
        Give us each day our daily bread.
        And forgive us our sins,
            for we ourselves forgive everyone
                indebted to us.
        And do not bring us to the time of trial."

LUKE 11:1-4

REMEMBER

If in contemplation I find in one or two words abundant matter for thought, I should not be anxious to go on.

62. Receive Jesus Often

Daily Communion was an unusual practice in the sixteenth century. Many Catholics received the sacrament only once or twice a year, as they thought themselves disqualified by their sins. Far ahead of his time, Ignatius encouraged the habit of daily Communion, in a letter to a holy nun who sought his advice.

As to daily Communion, we should recall that in the early Church everybody received daily, and that up to this time there has been no written ordinance of Holy Mother Church, nor objection by either positive or scholastic theologians against anyone receiving daily Communion should his devotion move him to do so. It is true that St. Augustine said that he would neither praise nor blame daily Communion, but he did, on the other hand, exhort everyone to receive on Sundays. Further on, speaking of the most sacred Body of Christ our Lord, he says: "This bread is our daily bread. So live, therefore, as to be able to receive it daily." . . . You may without doubt receive daily — in fact, it would be better for you to do so.

Letters 71-72

THINK ABOUT IT

■ Is it possible for me to get to Mass more often, perhaps on workdays?

- I will live in such a way that I may receive Jesus daily.
- I should be thankful for the privilege of frequent Communion.

JUST IMAGINE

So Jesus said to them, "Very truly, I tell you, unless you eat the flesh of the Son of Man and drink his blood, you have no life in you. Those who eat my flesh and drink my blood have eternal life, and I will raise them up on the last day; for my flesh is true food and my blood is true drink. Those who eat my flesh and drink my blood abide in me, and I in them. Just as the living Father sent me, and I live because of the Father, so whoever eats me will live because of me. This is the bread that came down from heaven, not like that which your ancestors ate, and they died. But the one who eats this bread will live forever."

JOHN 6:53-58

REMEMBER

This bread is our daily bread. So live, therefore, as to be able to receive it daily.

63. Say "Thanks"

Gratitude can be the beginning of inner peace and many virtues — and an antidote to many vices: pride, resentment, and wrath, to name just a few. St. Ignatius made the point in a letter to a Portuguese Jesuit.

It seems to me in the light of the Divine Goodness ... that ingratitude is the most abominable of sins and that it should be detested in the sight of our Creator and Lord by all of His creatures who are capable of enjoying His divine and everlasting glory. For it is a forgetting of the graces, benefits, and blessings received. As such it is the cause, beginning, and origin of all sins and misfortunes. On the contrary, the grateful acknowledgment of blessings and gifts received is loved and esteemed not only on earth but in heaven.

Letters 55

THINK ABOUT IT

- Ingratitude is the most abominable of sins, for it is a forgetting of the blessings received.
- I should keep a list of things for which I am thankful.
- I should say "thank you" many times a day, for all that pleases me and all that does not please me.

As [Jesus] entered a village, ten lepers approached him. Keeping their distance, they called out, saying, "Jesus, Master, have mercy on us!" When he saw them, he said to them, "Go and show yourselves to the priests." And as they went, they were made clean. Then one of them, when he saw that he was healed, turned back, praising God with a loud voice. He prostrated himself at Jesus' feet and thanked him. And he was a Samaritan. Then Jesus asked, "Were not ten made clean? But the other nine, where are they? Was none of them found to return and give praise to God except this foreigner?" LUKE 17:12-18

REMEMBER

Ingratitude is the cause, beginning, and origin of all sins and misfortunes.

64. Fair Wages!

Ignatius speaks of the high wages that God pays to His children; for, as brothers and sisters of Jesus, we share His dominion over all creation — even the angels! In our daily labors, we exercise that dominion, restoring God's order to the time and space we have been given.

His wage is everything you are and have in the natural order, for He bestows and preserves your being and life, and all the perfections of body and soul, as well as blessings that are eternal. His wage is also the spiritual gifts of His grace with which He has so generously and lovingly anticipated you and continues to offer even when you oppose Him and rebel against Him. His wage is also those incomparable blessings of His glory, which, without any advantage to Himself, He has promised you and holds in readiness for you, actually sharing with you all the treasures of His happiness, so that you may be — by a remarkable participation in His divine perfection — what He is by His essence and nature. Finally, His wage is the whole universe and everything material and spiritual it contains. For He has placed under our ministry, not only all that is under heaven but even the whole of His sublime court, not excepting even any of the heavenly hierarchy: "Are not all angels spirits in the divine service, sent to serve for the sake of those who are to inherit salvation?" (Hebrews 1:14).

As though this wage were not enough, He has made Himself our wage, becoming a brother in our own flesh, as the price of our salvation on the cross, and in the Eucharist to be with us as support and company. Oh, what an unworthy soldier he would be whom such a wage would not induce to labor for the honor of such a prince!

... How extremely ungrateful and hardhearted is he who after all this does not recognize his obligation to serve our Lord Jesus Christ diligently and to seek His honor.

Letters 124-125

THINK ABOUT IT

- God has given me everything I am and have.
- God has called me to share in His rule over all the earth.
- What return can I make to the Lord for all He has given me?

JUST IMAGINE

Blessed be the God and Father of our Lord Jesus Christ, who has blessed us in Christ with every spiritual blessing in the heavenly places.   EPHESIANS 1:3

REMEMBER

His wage is the whole universe and everything it contains. For He has placed under our ministry all that is under heaven, and even His heavenly court.

65. Cross Examination

It is good for us often to consider all that Jesus suffered for us. Some people keep a cross in their pocket during the workday. Some draw a small, inconspicuous cross and keep it where only they can see it.

Imagine Christ our Lord present before you upon the cross, and begin to speak with Him, asking how it is that, though He is the Creator, He has stooped to become man, and to pass from eternal life to death here in time, that thus He might die for our sins.

I shall also reflect upon myself and ask:

"What have I done for Christ?"
"What am I doing for Christ?"
"What ought I to do for Christ?"

As I behold Christ in this plight, nailed to the cross, I shall ponder upon what presents itself to my mind.

Exercises, n. 53

THINK ABOUT IT

■ I will find a way to remind myself often of the sacrifice of Jesus on the cross.

■ How is it that God — Who is infinite and eternal — became a mortal man?

■ When I do good things, do I tell Jesus I am doing them for Him?

He was despised and rejected by others;
a man of suffering and acquainted with
infirmity;
and as one from whom others hide their faces
he was despised, and we held him of no
account.
Surely he has borne our infirmities and carried our
diseases;
yet we accounted him stricken,
struck down by God, and afflicted.
But he was wounded for our transgressions,
crushed for our iniquities;
upon him was the punishment that made us whole,
and by his bruises we are healed. . . .
He was oppressed, and he was afflicted,
yet he did not open his mouth;
like a lamb that is led to the slaughter,
and like a sheep that before its shearers is silent,
so he did not open his mouth.
By a perversion of justice he was taken away.
Who could have imagined his future?
For he was cut off from the land of the living,
stricken for the transgression of my people.
They made his grave with the wicked
and his tomb with the rich,
although he had done no violence,
and there was no deceit in his mouth.

ISAIAH 53:3-5, 7-9

Christ died for my sins. What have I done for Christ?

66. Holy Indifference

One of the paradoxes of Christian life is that we must, in the words of one poet, learn "to care and not to care." We must care about the things of the world, because they are God's; but we must not be overattached to them or over-anxious about them, because they are not God Himself. Ignatius teaches us to accept what we have and to accept our losses as well.

Man is created to praise, reverence, and serve God our Lord, and by this means to save his soul.

Therefore, we must make ourselves indifferent to all created things, as far as we are allowed free choice and we are not under any prohibition. Consequently, as far as we are concerned, we should not prefer health to sickness, riches to poverty, honor to dishonor, a long life to a short life. The same holds for all other things.

Our one desire and choice should be what is more conducive to the end for which we are created.

Exercises, n. 23

THINK ABOUT IT

- I was created to praise, reverence, and serve God. This is how I must save my soul.
- I must learn to be indifferent to created things, even as I exercise just and loving stewardship over them for God's sake.

■ My one desire should be to fulfill the reason for my creation.

I have learned to be content with whatever I have. I know what it is to have little, and I know what it is to have plenty. In any and all circumstances I have learned the secret of being well-fed and of going hungry, of having plenty and of being in need. I can do all things through him who strengthens me.

PHILIPPIANS 4:11-13

We should not prefer health to sickness, riches to poverty, honor to dishonor, a long life to a short life.

67. The Things of This World

Ignatius wished his family to seek fulfillment in God alone, and not in the passing fashions and fortunes of the world. If we stake our joy on what we own, we'll never find lasting happiness.

It is none of my business to condemn a man who in this life lies awake with plans for adding to his buildings, his income, his estate, in the hope of leaving behind him a great name and reputation. But neither can I praise him; for, according to St. Paul, we ought to use the things of this world as though we used them not and own them as though we owned them not . . . because the fashion of this world passes and in a moment is gone.

Letters 7

THINK ABOUT IT

- I should neither praise nor condemn those who make ambitious plans for material gain.
- Do I look upon my good name and professional reputation as things of value only because they belong to God?
- The fashion of this world passes and in a moment is gone.

JUST IMAGINE

Then [Jesus] told them a parable: "The land of a rich man produced abundantly. And he thought to himself,

'What should I do, for I have no place to store my crops?' Then he said, 'I will do this: I will pull down my barns and build larger ones, and there I will store all my grain and my goods. And I will say to my soul, "Soul, you have ample goods laid up for many years; relax, eat, drink, be merry." ' But God said to him, 'You fool! This very night your life is being demanded of you. And the things you have prepared, whose will they be?' So it is with those who store up treasures for themselves but are not rich toward God."

LUKE 12:16-21

REMEMBER

We ought to use the things of this world as though we used them not and own them as though we owned them not.

Ignatius warned his friend Sister Teresa Rejadella that the devil would try to tempt her to keep silent about God's special graces to her.

When he sees someone so good and humble, ... [the devil] is ready with the suggestion that, should the Lord's servant happen to speak of the graces our Lord has bestowed upon him in actual deeds or merely in resolve or desire, he sins by another kind of vanity in speaking favorably of himself. In this way he tries to prevent him from speaking of any of the blessings he has received. His purpose is to prevent him from producing fruit in others as well as in himself. For he knows that, when such a person recalls to mind what he has received, he is always helped in regard to greater things. One ought, however, to be very reserved, and speak only with the motive of helping others or himself: others if he sees that they are in the proper dispositions and likely to believe him and draw some profit from what he says. Thus, when the enemy of our salvation sees that we are humble, he tries to draw us on to a humility that is excessive and counterfeit.

Letters 22

THINK ABOUT IT

- The devil wants to prevent us from producing spiritual fruit in others as well as in ourselves.

- We should be prudent in talking about God's gifts to us, but not necessarily silent.
- I should speak of graces only to those who are likely to believe and profit from my testimony.

It is necessary to boast; nothing is to be gained by it, but I will go on to visions and revelations of the Lord.... But if I wish to boast, I will not be a fool, for I will be speaking the truth. But I refrain from it, so that no one may think better of me than what is seen in me or heard from me, even considering the exceptional character of the revelations.

2 CORINTHIANS 12:1, 6-7

When the enemy sees that we are humble, he tries to draw us on to a humility that is excessive and counterfeit.

69. Give as God Has Given

This point from the Spiritual Exercises *ends with one of Ignatius's most famous prayers. The passage that begins "Take, Lord" serves well as a prayer of "morning offering."*

I will ponder with great affection how much God our Lord has done for me, and how much He has given me of what He possesses, and finally, how much, as far as He can, the same Lord desires to give Himself to me according to His divine decrees.

Then I will reflect upon myself, and consider, according to all reason and justice, what I ought to offer the Divine Majesty — that is, all I possess and myself with it. Thus, as one would do who is moved by great feeling, I will make this offering of myself:

> Take, Lord, and receive all my liberty, my memory, my understanding, and my entire will, all that I have and possess. You have given all to me. To You, O Lord, I return it. All is Yours, dispose of it wholly according to Your will. Give me Your love and Your grace, for this is sufficient for me.

Exercises, n. 234

THINK ABOUT IT

■ Do I make a complete offering of myself to God, or do I hold something back?

- What in my life do I cling to most greedily, as if it belonged to me and not to God?
- I will resolve to begin each day with a prayer of "morning offering," as soon as I rise from bed.

JUST IMAGINE

"For this reason the Father loves me, because I lay down my life in order to take it up again. No one takes it from me, but I lay it down of my own accord. I have power to lay it down, and I have power to take it up again. I have received this command from my Father."   JOHN 10:17-18

REMEMBER

I will ponder with great affection how much God our Lord has done for me.

70. Prayer Goes to Work

Few people knew the mind and heart of Ignatius as well as his companion and secretary Father Jerome Nadal. He commented, below, that Ignatian prayer — the prayer of the Society of Jesus — properly results in action, service, and execution: it goes to work.

The operative principle and the end of prayer is love. That is only to say that prayer tends to the greater glory of God by proceeding from the fullness of love, in such fashion that I should desire by my prayer what I ask and seek to obtain, in order to serve God more according to the vocation and Institute of the Society. Accordingly, the prayer of the Society favors execution.

Modern 152

THINK ABOUT IT

- The beginning of prayer is love.
- The end of prayer is love.
- My prayer should lead me to active service of God and neighbor.

JUST IMAGINE

Be doers of the word, and not merely hearers.... Those who look into the perfect law, the law of liberty, and persevere, being not hearers who forget but doers who act — they will be blessed in their doing.

JAMES 1:22, 25

The operative principle and the end of prayer is love.

71. The Circle of Service and Prayer

Prayer is sterile unless it leads to service. Service is ineffective unless it proceeds from prayer. For the Christian at work in the world, these two elements are inseparable and interdependent. The following reflection comes from Ignatius's close companion Father Jerome Nadal.

This is what I would like to call the circle of occupations.... If you are occupied with your neighbor and with the service of God in your ministry or in any office, God will help you afterwards more efficaciously in your prayer. And this more effective divine aid will in turn enable you to take care of your neighbor with more courage and spiritual profit.

Modern 153

THINK ABOUT IT

- In my life, do I close the circle — completing prayer with service, and service with prayer?
- Do I begin my works with prayer, so that they are oriented toward God?
- Do I pray every day for the people I am serving through my work — my customers, employers, employees, and co-workers?

JUST IMAGINE

Show me your faith apart from your works, and I by my works will show you my faith.... Was not our ancestor Abraham justified by works when he offered his son Isaac on the altar? You see that faith was active along with his works, and faith was brought to completion by the works. . . . You see that a person is justified by works and not by faith alone. . . . For just as the body without the spirit is dead, so faith without works is also dead.   JAMES 2:18, 21-22, 24, 26

REMEMBER

This is the circle of occupations: Be occupied with service, and God will help you in your prayer. Your prayer will in turn empower you for service.

72. Contemplation in Action

The following testimony comes from Father Jerome Nadal, a close colleague and sometime secretary to Ignatius. Ignatius was immersed in his daily work, but no less immersed in God.

Father Ignatius, we know, received from God the unique grace of great facility in the contemplation of the Most Holy Trinity. This gift of contemplative prayer he received in a very singular manner towards the end of his years on earth, although he had enjoyed it frequently also at other times. At that period, however, he possessed it to such a degree that in all things, in every action or conversation, he was aware of God's presence and felt so great a taste for spiritual things as to be lost in their contemplation. In a word he was . . . contemplative even while engaged in action, a habit that he was accustomed to explain while remarking: "God must be found in all things."

Modern 149

THINK ABOUT IT

- In all things, in every action or conversation, Ignatius was aware of God's presence.
- Like Ignatius, I should strive to be a contemplative even while engaged in action.
- I must work to cultivate a "taste for spiritual things."

It is no longer I who live, but it is Christ who lives in me. And the life I now live in the flesh I live by faith in the Son of God, who loved me and gave himself for me.   GALATIANS 2:20

Ignatius was contemplative even while engaged in action, a habit he was accustomed to explain while remarking: "God must be found in all things."

73. Aim High

Ignatius reminded his companions that God had given them great gifts, so they should give Him great works in return. Slipshod work is an unworthy offering to God.

No commonplace achievement will satisfy the great obligations you have of excelling. If you consider the nature of your vocation, you will see that what would not be slight in others would be slight in you. . . . Direct your thoughts and affections and employ them in attaining the end for which God created you — that is, His own honor and glory, your own salvation, and the help of your neighbor.

Letters 122

THINK ABOUT IT

- Considering what God has given me, I must hold myself to a higher standard.
- I must be ambitious to glorify God by doing my work well.
- God has made me for this reason: to glorify Him, to be saved, and to help my neighbor.

JUST IMAGINE

"From everyone to whom much has been given, much will be required; and from the one to whom much has been entrusted, even more will be demanded."

LUKE 12:48

No commonplace achievement will do. What would not be slight in others would be slight in you.

74. A.M.D.G.

Ignatius's motto was Ad Maiorem Dei Gloriam *("To the Greater Glory of God"). When he began a piece of writing, he first inscribed those four initials at the top of the page. They represented his reason for working and his reason for living.*

To the greater glory of God!

THINK ABOUT IT

- At the beginning of every task, I should rededicate myself to God.
- Whose glory do I seek in my work?
- How might God be glorified in my labors — in my successes and my failures?

JUST IMAGINE

And this is my prayer, that your love may overflow more and more with knowledge and full insight to help you to determine what is best, so that in the day of Christ you may be pure and blameless, having produced the harvest of righteousness that comes through Jesus Christ for the glory and praise of God.

PHILIPPIANS 1:9-11

REMEMBER

A.M.D.G. — *Ad Maiorem Dei Gloriam* — To the Greater Glory of God!

Action, 8, 25, 40, 48, 91, 161, 165-166

Affection, 42, 43, 54-55, 75, 89, 159-160, 167

Afterlife, 85-86

Almsgiving, 10

Ambition (see also Goals), 13, 35, 49

Angels, 92, 148

Anger, 19, 81-82, 87

Annoyance, 73, 106

Anxiety, 122-123

Ardor, 46

Attachments, worldly, 8, 56, 66

Authority (see also Obedience), 23-24, 54-55, 87, 103

Blame, 108, 126, 144

Charity, 22, 52, 54, 64-65, 72-73, 87, 98-99, 116, 129

Cheating, 75

Cheerfulness, 62, 79-80

Church, 12-13, 55, 96, 102, 144

Comfort, 23, 72, 110-111, 120

Communion, Holy, 140, 144-145

Complacency, 46

Confession, 15, 17, 64, 130, 140

Consolation, 25, 62, 72, 79-80, 106, 120-121, 142

Consulting others, 68-69, 129

Contemplation, 8, 25, 142-143, 165-166

Conversation, 12, 37, 40, 58, 165

Correcting others (fraternal correction), 23, 52, 54-55, 58, 129-130

Courage, 25, 102, 106-107, 110-111, 163

Creation, 22-23, 26, 148, 154

Criticism, critics, 74, 129

Cutting corners, 75, 167

Death, 35, 64, 91-93, 130, 150

Decision making, 68-69

Defects (faults), 54-55, 74, 76, 118, 129, 130, 139

Depression, 72

Desire, 23, 29-32, 37, 48-49, 56-57, 67, 83-84, 94, 120, 129, 133, 153-154, 157, 159, 161

Detachment, 23

Details, 38

Devil, 35-36, 120-121, 157

Discretion, 48

Dissatisfaction, 17, 23, 56, 81

Dominion, mankind's, over creation, 148

Embarrassment (shame), 124

Ends, 22, 66-67, 77, 153, 161-162, 167

Evangelization, 83

Example to others, 29-30, 79, 87, 100, 106, 114, 124, 157-158

Excess, 48, 60, 112, 157-158

Flattery, 60-61

Fortitude, 33, 110

Freedom (liberty), 159, 161

Friends, friendship, 10, 21, 23-24, 42, 54, 60-61, 72, 74, 83, 116, 129-130, 133, 157

Generosity, 33, 44, 75, 85-86, 92, 98, 148

Gifts from God, 31-32, 77, 98, 104, 114-115, 133, 137, 146, 148, 158, 165, 167

Glory, 8, 10, 16, 22, 25-26, 29-30, 35-37, 42-43, 64, 75, 83-84, 91-92, 114, 140-141, 146, 148, 161, 167, 169

Goals (see also Ambition), 10-11, 19, 22, 35, 38, 67

Gossip, 75

Gratitude, 146

Habit, 21, 62, 116, 139, 144, 165-166

Happiness, 30, 72, 148, 155

Health, physical, 42, 114-116, 153-154

Heaven, 22, 35-36, 76, 85-88, 96-97, 110, 125, 131, 136, 145-146, 148-149

Hell, 53

Holy Name of Jesus, 19, 24, 29, 40, 81, 100, 110

Humility, 24, 31-32, 48-49, 65, 98-99, 108, 124, 126, 157-158

Idleness, 46, 50, 77-78, 100-101

Image of God, human beings as, 23, 29-30, 48, 139

Imagination in prayer, 12, 24-25

Influence, 42, 85

Intellectual formation, 46

Intention, 38, 52, 54, 64, 66-67, 122, 127, 133

Jesus, devotion to, 24, 33

Judging others, 52, 74, 91

Kindness, 56, 58, 77, 129

Laziness, 46-47, 62-63

Listening, 50-51, 55-58, 68-69, 74

Love for God, 23-24, 38, 46, 83, 85, 106-107, 140

Love for others, 23, 57, 83, 89-90, 96, 106

Management, 19, 68

Marriage, 66-67

Mass, 19, 33, 144

Means, 23, 62, 66-67, 77, 102-103, 153

Meditation, 10-12, 40

Menial work, 98

Method, Ignatian, 10, 21, 24-26, 40, 68, 122, 142

Moderation, 112-113

Money, 22, 35, 60, 85, 87, 89, 102, 104

Morning offering, 159-160

Motives, 37, 43, 75, 157

Negative speech, 74-78

Negotiation, 50, 79

Obedience (see also Authority), 23-24, 96, 114, 126

Opposition, 106

Passion, 13-14, 29-30, 62, 81

Paycheck, 89

Peace, 17, 22, 48, 62-63, 81, 146

Peacemaker, 81

Perfection, 54, 91, 118, 126, 128, 148

Perseverance, 33, 106-107, 161

Planning, 44, 104, 155

Politeness, 50

Pope, 19, 24, 42, 44, 96, 102

Positive speech, 17, 42, 48, 50-51, 56-59, 79, 81, 94-95, 129, 157-158

Possessions, 77, 104

Posture, 48, 143

Prayer, 8, 11-12, 17, 19-20, 24-26, 33, 37, 40, 67, 76, 96, 121-122, 126, 131, 133-134, 136-137, 140, 142-143, 159-165, 169

Preferences, personal, 72-73

Presence of God, 11, 26, 40-41, 135-136, 165

Pride, 48, 127, 146

Procrastination, 44-45

Progress, spiritual, 126-127, 130, 133

Prosperity (abundance), 85-88

Punctuality, 70-71

Raise, asking for a, 102-103

Rash judgment, 52-53

Reprimand, 87

Resentment, 81, 146

Respect for others, 48, 56, 87

Retreat, spiritual, 24, 133

Scandal, 58, 94-95, 124

Schedule, 12, 70, 133

Self-knowledge, 24, 120-121, 124

Self-love (selfishness), 22, 23, 62, 126

Service, 12, 17, 19, 22-23, 25, 37, 62-66, 70-71, 75, 83-84, 89, 102-103, 106, 108, 116-117, 128, 133, 148, 161, 163-164

Sickness, 18, 72, 92, 114-115, 117, 153-154

Sin, 17, 23-24, 33, 54-55, 60-62, 74, 77-78, 102, 110, 124-125, 129-130, 135, 138-139, 143-144, 146-147, 150-152, 157

Speaking plainly, 131-132

Study, 18, 24, 31, 37, 64-65, 96, 110-111, 137

Subordinates, 50

Suffering, 16, 18, 72-73, 76, 108, 114, 120-121, 150-151

Temperament, differences in, 42-43, 56-57

Thinking before speaking, 42-43, 50-59, 74, 77-78, 94-95, 131-132

Thinking with the Church, 23-24, 96-97

Truth, 40, 60-61, 84, 158

Wages, 102, 148-149

Will, God's, 23-24, 29, 33, 38, 62, 64-65, 67, 110, 118, 159

Words, 21, 29, 42, 48, 75-79, 114, 135-136, 138, 142-143, 153

Work, unpleasant or difficult, 22, 44-45, 70-71, 98-99, 106-107

Workaholism, 12, 26, 112-113, 116-117

World, 8-9, 17, 20, 22-23, 25-26, 29-30, 35-36, 63, 75-76, 87-89, 92, 117, 136, 153, 155-156, 163

MIKE AQUILINA, vice-president of the St. Paul Center for Biblical Theology, has authored or edited more than a dozen books on Catholic history, doctrine, and devotion, including the best-selling *What Catholics Believe.* He is currently co-host of EWTN's *Swear to God* and a regular panelist on *The Weekly Roman Observer* broadcast by the Catholic Family Network.

FATHER KRIS D. STUBNA received his doctorate in theology from the Pontifical Gregorian University in Rome. He is the diocesan secretary for education for the Diocese of Pittsburgh. Father Stubna is the author or co-author of several books, including *A Pocket Catechism for Kids.*

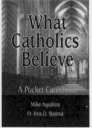